# STEPFATHERS ARE PEOPLE TOO

BY D.L. STEWART

ILLUSTRATIONS BY FRANK PAUER

Have a laugh on me.

D L Stewart

***Other Tales From The Paternity Ward By D.L. Stewart:***

***The Man In The Blue Flannel Pajamas***

***Fathers Are People Too***

***Father Knows Best—Sometimes***

***Stepfathers Are People Too***
***D.L. Stewart***


45 S. Ludlow St.
Dayton, OH 45402

For

Adam

His short, sweet song
still lingers in our hearts.

# THIS BOOK IS FOR AMERICA'S 13 MILLION STEPFATHERS

- But it also is for stepmothers.
- And for "regular" parents.
- For kids and for stepkids.
- For grandparents and for in-laws.
- For aunts and uncles and nieces and nephews and cousins.
- And cats.
- In short, it is for anyone who is — or ever has been — a member of a family.

## *Table of Contents*

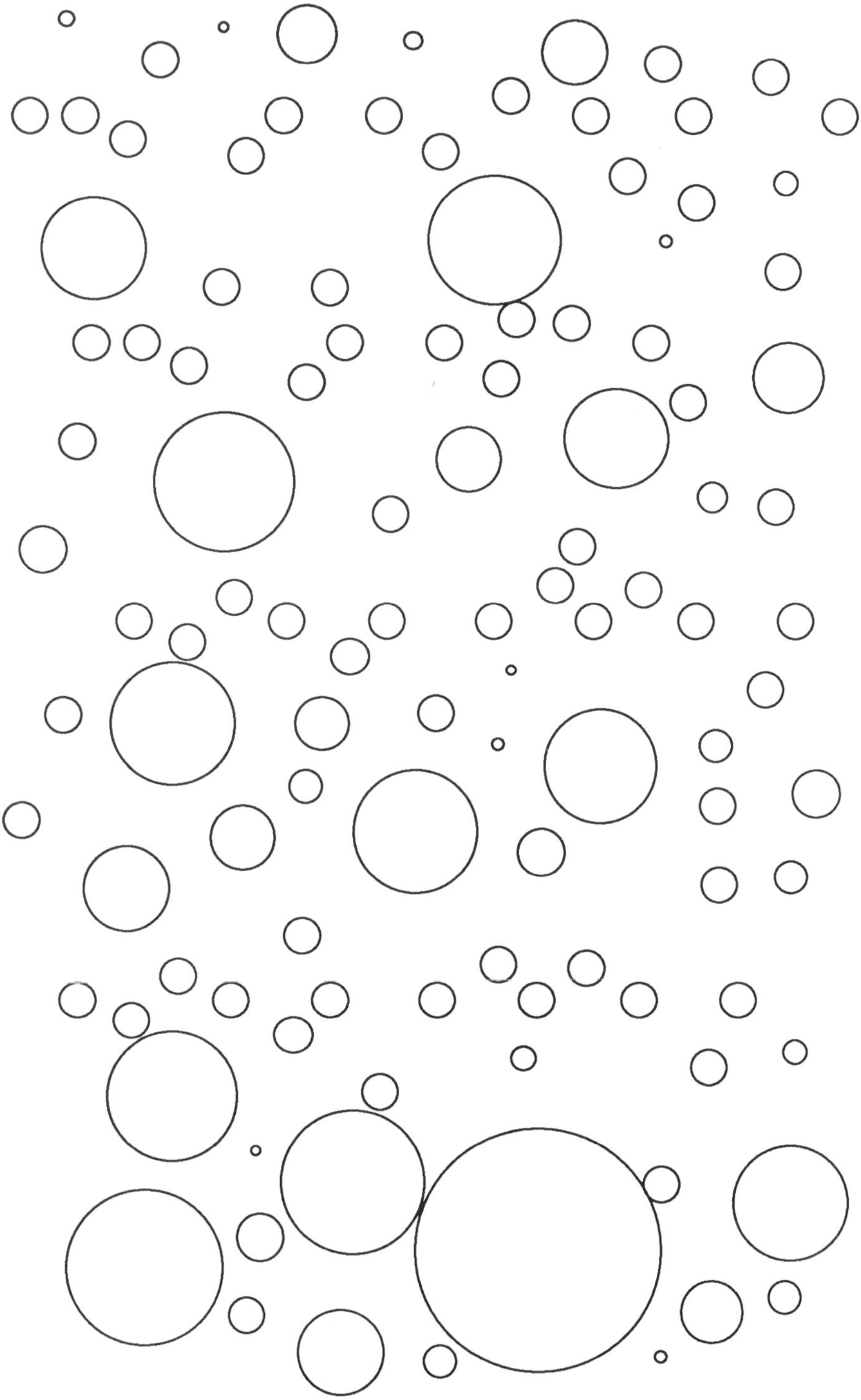

PREFACE: CHAPTER 1

# THE STORM BEFORE THE CALM

In our bliss, which was total, and our ignorance, which was monumental, we just sort of assumed that our families would be a perfect blend.

She had two sons, aged 10 and 13. I had two sons, aged 12 and 15. The mix couldn't be more ideal, we agreed as we made plans to retrace our steps down the aisle. They would play touch football together. They would trade baseball cards. They would stay awake long after their bedtimes, whispering crude juvenile jokes and making disgusting bodily noises. They would develop a bond of boyhood. I could almost picture one of mine carrying one of hers on his back and saying, "He ain't heavy, he's my stepbrother."

We probably should have realized it wasn't necessarily going to be that way on the day I told my 12-year-old that our two households soon were to become one and he responded, "Cool. I've always wanted a little brother to beat up."

At the very latest, we should have had our doubts when we had to interrupt the wedding ceremony three times to break up rice fights between her boys and mine.

In the year that followed, our sons grew older, but no closer. The days on which we had custody of all four of them were marked on our calendar as "Wrestlemania." None of mine ever carried one of hers on his back, although one of hers did step on the head of one of mine during a particularly vicious argument over whose turn it was to say grace.

The absence of stepbrotherly love seemed to bother my wife more than it bothered me. But then, we had different attitudes about child-raising.

She got upset when they raised their voices to each other. I figured there was no need to get involved until I heard the sound of gunfire.

"Face it," I pointed out, "brotherhood isn't a relationship, it's a survival course. It's always been that way, even for natural brothers. Cain and Abel didn't get along real well and they didn't even have video games to argue about."

"I don't care," she said. "I can't stand it. This isn't a family, it's an adolescent tag-team match."

"I don't think there's much we can do about it. What we've got here are new family dynamics complicating your basic sibling rivalry."

"Don't tell me about sibling rivalry," she countered. "My sister and I never had to resort to physical violence to settle our problems."

"Girls are different. They don't punch each other. They just do nasty things to each other's sweaters and say mean things about their hairdos."

"Well, I think we need to have a family meeting to talk about this."

She summoned them to the kitchen, but the meeting was doomed before it began. There were four boys and only two empty chairs. Her 11-year-old grabbed one chair. Her 14-year-old took the other. When my 16-year-old arrived, he saw there were no chairs left. So he sat on her 14-year-old. My 13-year-old walked into the kitchen last, noticed there was a chair shortage and knocked the 11-year-old onto the floor.

The family symposium on peace and brotherhood had begun with two kids on one chair, wrestling. A 13-year-old on another chair, grinning. An 11-year-old on the floor, bawling. Family unity was not going to be easy to sell to this crowd.

"The reason we're calling this meeting," I began, after chaos had been reduced to simple disorderly conduct, "is to talk about the fighting you guys are doing. We realize it's not an easy situation when two families are learning to adjust to each other, but I'm sure we're all mature enough to understand the need for cooperation and . . . "

The rest of my speech was drowned out by a brawl that erupted when her 11-year-old got off the floor and attacked my 13-year-old.

And then it happened.

*My* 16-year-old jumped off his chair and came to the aid of *her* 11-year-old. An instant later, *her* 14-year-old was helping *my* 13-year-old.

We stood in the kitchen doorway, my wife and I, watching our sons punching, kicking, scratching and screaming. It was a magic moment.

I slipped my arm around her waist.

"You know what this means, don't you?" I asked.

She looked up at me and nodded. A small tear had formed in the corner of her eye.

"We're a family now," she sniffled.

# CHAPTER 1

O

It's scarier the second time around.

The first time the wedding bells ring, their sound is sweet and pure and dazzlingly, dizzyingly, clear. Sometimes they ring so loudly they drown out some sounds you should be hearing. They deafen you to the statistics about divorce and punctured dreams and love stories grown cold. Those are just numbers, you tell yourself as the bells are ringing in your ears. They are misfortunes that happen to other people. They have nothing to do with your love, which is unprecedented, unrivaled and predestined to live forever.

That's the way most first marriages begin. The way, perhaps, they must begin.

It's not that way with second marriages.

If and when the bells ring again, the sweet sound is muted by reality. Certainty is tempered by experience. Life, and love, no longer seem dazzlingly clear. You have been a statistic. Dreams have been punctured and the love story you assumed would be eternal ended several years short of happily ever after.

But the bells *do* ring again. More than nine million households in this country contain at least one partner who has been there before. Twenty-two percent of those families have children from one or both of the first marriages.

After 22 years of marriage (which produced four kids), and three years of the dating game (which produced none), I hear the bells ringing for me again.

Her name is Miriam. But her friends, of which she has several million who phone her every day, call her Mimi. She is petite and blond and lovely. She is a schoolteacher. She smiles a lot and laughs a lot and loves to cook and to entertain. She has a cat. (I never said the woman was perfect.)

Like me, she has been married once before. Like me, she shares custody of two sons, neither of whom is involved in any activity within walking distance of home.

As in any relationship, there are differences. But we knew that going in.

Our religious backgrounds are not the same. She is Jewish. I am not.

Some of her friends own their own companies. A lot of my friends own their own television sets. But there is some comfort in knowing that she didn't marry me for my money.

The first time I visit her condo, I discover that she has a coffee table full of fashion magazines and a walk-in closet stuffed with enough clothes to overwhelm Diana Ross. I have four *Sports Illustrated* swimsuit editions in the backseat of my Chevy and I tend to think of clothes merely as something to keep you from getting arrested for indecent exposure.

Then there are the differences that test the relationship of every man and woman.

There is dirt, for instance.

I wouldn't necessarily want to get into a debate with Murphy Brown about this, but I have reason to believe that there are certain unalterable differences between men and women on the subject of dirt.

It could be physical, something along the lines of the differences in pelvic structures. It may be that women are born with some sort of extra lens in their eyes that enables them to see a speck of spaghetti sauce on a necktie that a man could not see without the aid of an electron microscope.

Or maybe it's nature's way of compensating. The average woman does not have the upper body strength to hit a baseball 420 feet, nature may have reasoned. So let's give her the ability to sit behind home plate and notice that the centerfielder has a Gatorade stain on his sock.

Not only are there women who can actually see bacteria, I know several who can *hear* them.

I like to think I have a pretty average male relationship with dirt. If I happen to come across an amount of dirt that appears to be life-threatening, I will clean it up. But I see no reason to go out of my way to look for it.

Most of the women I have known, on the other chromosome, seem dedicated to the goal of stamping out dirt in our lifetime. My ex-wife and I never could agree on what constituted a "filthy mess." She considered a smudge on the patio window to be the first step toward a visit from the Board of Health. I figured if it wasn't bigger than the Exxon Valdez oil spill, it probably wasn't worth worrying about.

The first time she comes to my apartment for dinner I realize that life with my future wife won't be much different, dirt-wise.

In preparation for her visit, I have swept, dusted, waxed and polished the entire apartment. It has taken me practically a whole halftime to get the job done.

When she arrives, she hands me her coat, takes a quick sniff and says:

"Dinner smells great. I love fried chicken."

"Then you should have been here two weeks ago," I tell her. "I haven't started cooking tonight's dinner yet."

I fix her a drink and head for the kitchen. As I am chipping rice from the bottom of the pan, she calls from the living room.

"I'd like to freshen up a little bit. Mind if I use the bathroom?"

"Of course not. But be sure to use mine and not the 19-year-old's. I haven't had a chance to clean it since he went back to college."

"Which one is the 19-year-old's?"

"The one with the padlock and the nasty note from the EPA nailed to the door. Oh, and the white towel is for guests."

A few minutes later she appears in the kitchen.

"I didn't see any white towels," she says, "so I used a gray one. Is that all right?"

"Perfect," I reply.

"Is there anything I can do to help you?"

"No, thanks. Things are pretty well under control."

"How about if I clear those dirty breakfast dishes off the table and set it for dinner?"

"It *is* set for dinner."

I turn my attention back to the stove. When it is time to take the rolls out of the oven, I ask her to hand me the oven mitts that are on the counter behind her. She picks one of them up between her thumbnail and fingernail and holds it at arm's length as if it were a three-week-old pork chop.

"Is there a problem?" I ask.

"Well, I don't mean to pry, but how long has it been since you've washed this thing?"

"Wash it? It's a potholder, for crying out loud. I don't use it for performing open heart surgery."

When dinner is finished, she starts to carry the dishes to the kitchen.

"Don't worry about those," I tell her. "I'll do them later."

Actually, I wouldn't mind having her do the dishes with me. But I know if she gets a close look at the inside of my sink, the relationship is doomed.

If meeting my potholder is her first big test, getting acquainted with her cat is mine.

On the evening we met, she told me immediately that she was divorced.

"No problem," I replied, "so am I."

When I called to ask her for a date a few days later, she informed me that she had two kids.

"That's fine," I said. "I have four, and two of them are with me on weekends."

As I was driving her home from our first date, she mentioned that she had a cat.

"How about if I drop you off at the next corner and you catch a bus?" I suggested.

It's not that I don't like cats, exactly. It's just that I haven't quite figured out why they were invented. Cats are not big enough to hitch to a plow. They are not loyal enough to run 40 miles through a blizzard with a keg of brandy around their necks. They don't even taste good. Probably.

What cats do, mostly, is sit on your furniture, walk across your face while you are sleeping and leave fragments of small, dead animals on your doorstep.

Her cat, I quickly discover, has one additional skill. He is the greatest escape artist since Houdini.

I first learn of her cat's talent when I go to her condo to pick her up for a date. As we are about to leave the house, I ask if I can use her bathroom.

"The cat's in there," she says.

"Well, can I use it when he's done?"

"You don't understand, he's not *using* the bathroom. I had to put him in there before I could open the front door to let you in. Otherwise he would have slipped outside and been gone all night."

"What's wrong with that? It's natural for cats to want to be outside. I think it has to do with their instinctive urge to hunt."

"I don't think he goes out there to hunt. He's been declawed."

"Then it probably has to do with his instinctive urge to . . . "

"He's been neutered, too."

"The only other possibility is that he goes bar-hopping. Check his breath the next time he comes home. Anyway, I can't believe you go to all the trouble of catching the cat and locking him in the bathroom every time you want to open the front door. Why don't you just outsmart him?"

"He's pretty fast and sneaky."

"Maybe. But he's just a dumb animal. We, on the other hand, are members of the species with the highest intelligence on earth. Come on, I'll prove it to you. Let him out of the bathroom and I'll show you how to handle this."

While she goes to let the cat out of the bathroom, I get a piece of his favorite kitty treat from the cupboard. To get a piece of this stuff, she has assured me, that cat would dance with a pit bulldog.

"Now, when we're ready to go out, I'll toss the snack down the hallway into the kitchen," I explain. "When he runs after it, we'll just open the door and slip out."

We stand at the front door. I hurl a piece of the kitty treat into the kitchen. The cat runs after it. We slip out the front door and walk to my car. When we get there, the cat is sitting behind the steering wheel. With kitty treat crumbs on his whiskers.

Before our next date, I come up with another plan.

"You go to the front door and pretend you're going out," I tell her. "Then, while he's watching you, I'll sneak out the back door."

"Great," she says. "But then how do I get out?"

"I didn't say this plan was perfect."

For the next several months, the battle with my future stepcat rages on. It would be simplest, I suppose, merely to lock him in the bathroom the way she used to. But I refuse to concede that I can't outwit an animal that needs three companies of firefighters to get him out of a tree.

Besides, I have high hopes for my next plan. The tricky part will be getting her to agree to tear her bedsheets into strips so we can make a rope and hang it out her bedroom window.

Meeting her kids is easier than meeting her cat. Probably because neither of them attempts to dash outside when I open her front door.

Neither of them, in fact, bothers to take his eyes off the television screen the first time they are there when I come to pick her up for a date.

"Boys," she says, leading me into the living room, "say hello to D.L."

"Uh," the 13-year-old grunts, continuing to stare at the screen.

"You gonna marry my mom?" the 10-year-old demands.

"No. I thought I'd just move in with her for a while, swindle her out of all her money and then dump her for a younger woman," I reply. When you're dealing with 10-year-olds, honesty is the best policy.

"Uh," he says.

Their mother goes upstairs to finish putting on her makeup, leaving the three of us alone in the living room. They ignore me and continue to watch television. In the midst of ignoring me, the 13-year-old emits a small, but distinct, belch. The 10-year-old sneaks a glance at me out of the corner of his eye to see how I will react. Instinct tells me there is only one thing to do at this point.

Opening my mouth, I expel a deep, rumbling response that lasts a full three seconds and sounds something like "BAAARF."

"Awesome," the 13-year-old exclaims, turning to look at me for the first time.

"How'd you do that?" the 10-year-old marvels, clearly impressed.

"I learned it in college," I admit, modestly. "I had a roommate who could rip an entire sentence."

By the time their mother comes back downstairs her sons and I have developed the kind of rapport that can only be described as "gut level."

As we leave for our date, the 10-year-old shouts after us, "Hey, don"t forget to marry my mom."

I am, of course, pleased that he has accepted me so readily. Even though I know he'd be more impressed if she married my former college roommate. And, to be honest, I would have had mixed reactions if she did.

Maybe beggars can't be choosers, but when I re-entered the dating game I was determined to hold out for a few simple criteria. The woman of my choice, I decided, would be personable, intelligent, reasonably attractive, born in this century, have no children and live within a reasonable distance of my apartment.

She was personable, intelligent, very attractive and five years younger than I. On the other hand, there were those two kids. And her condo, which was four ZIP codes away.

But the bells already had begun to ring.

Not that I could hear them right away, of course. Not until the tennis tournament.

It is a charity fund-raising event, one of those social events where you pay an entry fee, play mixed doubles with a person you have never met before, take a break for drinks and nibbles, play another set with another person you have never met before, take another break, play another set. By the end of the evening, everyone has gained 10 pounds, no one remembers the scores and a few players have to be carried home in their Prince bags.

No one takes tournaments like those seriously. Except for the people who win them. Which, as the evening progresses, appears as if it might be me.

What you have to understand here is that winning tennis tournaments is not something I do every day. It is not, in fact, something I do *any* day. In half a dozen years of double faulting, I never have won a tennis tournament. There have been years in which I have not won my serve.

This time, though, it's different. In the first round I draw a partner who hits the ball like Jennifer Capriati and we win 11 of 14 games. When the match is finished, I stroll over to the scoreboard, where I discover that I am the leader in the men's division. I pop open a beer and nibble a handful of pretzels. No sense getting all worked up about this thing. The odds are good that I will get wiped out in the second round. Besides, it's only a meaningless little tournament.

But in the second round I draw a partner who hits the ball like Martina Navratilova and we win seven of 11 games. When the match is finished, I grab a beer and race to the scoreboard, where I discover that I am leading by two games in the men's division. I pour out the rest of my beer and gulp a handful of steroids. This is no time to be drinking. I am on the verge of victory in one of the major events of the tennis tour.

I return to the court for the third round. My new partner already is warming up. She hits the ball like Queen Kong. I'm gonna win this thing.

The signal is given for the match to begin. Before my partner can toss the ball for her first serve, I hear a voice on the loudspeaker announcing that there is a phone call for me. I excuse myself and run to the phone.

"This is Good Samaritan Hospital," a voice on the other end of the line says. The woman I have been dating has been in an auto accident, the voice informs me.

"Oh my gosh, how is she?" I ask, dropping my tennis racquet and fumbling for my car keys. In that moment, all thoughts of the tennis tournament disappear from my mind, replaced by a picture of her in the emergency room, fighting for her life.

"She's all right," the voice says. "She just has some arm and leg injuries."

In that moment, several thoughts of the tennis tournament reappear, forming a split-screen image in my mind: My partner is waiting on the court. The woman I am dating is lying in the emergency room. We are 45 minutes from victory. I am 30 minutes from the hospital.

If I stay and play, I will feel like a heel for not rushing to her side. On the other hand, the voice assured me that she isn't seriously hurt. When's the last time you read about anyone dying from arm and leg injuries?

If I stay and win this tournament, there probably will be a trophy, which I can display in my apartment to remind me of this night. On the other hand, if I stay and win this tournament, my trophy and I will have plenty of time to sit alone in my apartment and stare at each other.

I pick up my racquet. I zip it into my tennis bag. I find my car keys. As I head for the parking lot, I hear the faint sound of ringing bells.

When I reach the hospital, I find that the voice was right. Her car was totaled, but she has only minor injuries. My car and I, on the other hand, may never recover.

The excitement starts on the Monday following the accident, when we both have custody of our respective kids for the next week. She calls me at work and mentions that, without a car, she has no way to pick them up after Hebrew school.

"Well, I guess I could get them," I say. "What time are they finished?"

"The 10-year-old is done at 6 o'clock."

"That'll work. I'll pick up my 15-year-old after wrestling, drive across town and pick up your kids, then drive back to my end of town and pick up my 12-year-old from basketball practice. Then we can all have dinner together."

"Except for my 13-year-old," she says.

"Why, is he on a diet?"

"He doesn't get out of Hebrew school until 8."

That evening I pick up my 15-year-old at the high school, put him in the front seat and drive across town to pick up her 10-year-old at Hebrew school. I put him in the back seat, drive back across town and pick up my 12-year-old at the junior high. I put him in the back seat, drive back across town and pick up her 13-year-old at Hebrew school. I stack him in the back seat on top of my 12-year-old and we all drive to her condo singing the theme from *The Brady Bunch*. By the time I get my kids home, it is 10:30 and my car has 143 new miles on the odometer.

On Tuesday I repeat the routine. By Wednesday I have picked up so many kids at so many schools that I am giving serious consideration to painting my car yellow and having a sign installed on the back warning that it is illegal to pass me when I am stopped.

"You know," I mention between pickups on Thursday, "I've spent so much time driving kids around that I haven't had much time to be with you. But the good thing is that our kids are getting to know each other. My 12-year-old really seems to be enjoying it."

"He probably likes the fact that he's not the youngest," she says.

"Yeah. And my 13-year-old said . . . "

"The 13-year-old is mine," she says.

"Are you sure?"

"Positive. He's the one getting ready for his *bar mitzvah*. Yours is the 15-year-old who's trying to qualify for the district wrestling tournament."

"Well, I hope your kid knows how to get out of a half-nelson. I think I just dropped him off at wrestling practice."

"Maybe we should call the school and find out," she suggests.

"Don't bother. If my 15-year-old says *shalom* when he gets into the car, we'll know."

Two weeks after the accident, she still hasn't been able to find a new car. I don't want to rush her, but finally I mention that she might want to start hitting a few showrooms.

"All this driving around is wearing out my car and it's getting your kids confused," I point out. "You'll never guess what your 10-year-old called me when he got out of my car this afternoon."

"Oh, no. He didn't call you 'Dad,' did he?"

"Nope. He called me 'cabbie.' "

By now the bells are too loud to ignore. *"Go for it,'"* they are saying. *"She is a wonderful woman. You are in love. Your kids do not love each other, but they aren't pulling knives on each other, either. Besides, your car's transmission is just about shot."*

So I pop the question, she pops the answer, we set a wedding date and I try to figure out how to break the news to my teen-agers.

Among the myriad delusions of parenthood is the one about how our kids spend a significant amount of their mental energies thinking about us. And that what we do is of vital interest to them.

I'm not sure where an idea like that got started. My best guess is that it either was a theory postulated by an unmarried child psychologist or by a scriptwriter for *Father Knows Best.* And I'm willing to bet that not even Princess and Bud knew the name of their father's boss.

The reality is that kids are so wrapped up in their own lives they don't have time to worry about what their parents are doing.

It's universal.

When the first Soviet cosmonaut returned from space, his kid probably said, "So, where were you, out of town or something?"

What an adult considers big news seldom will get much reaction out of a kid unless it has a direct bearing on his allowance. The last time any major event in my life was considered worth turning down the volume on the stereo for was the day I bought a new car. As I pulled into the driveway, two of them raced out the front door and said, "Nice car, Dad. Can you drive us to the mall?"

Knowing all that, I can't imagine why I am even remotely surprised at the way my middle son greets the announcement of my upcoming marriage. If nothing else, I should have remembered the way he reacted when I got divorced.

Telling the kids about the divorce was the part their mother and I dreaded the most. We approached it with care and concern. We consulted experts and read literature. We spent hours discussing what we would say, what we wouldn't say and how best to reassure all our children that they were not to blame and that we still loved them as much as ever.

When we had finished telling them, there was a long moment of silence before our middle son finally reacted.

"Can I turn the television back on now?" he demanded.

Psychologists at this very moment, I am sure, are stroking their beards and murmuring, "Classic denial and repression symptoms. Keep an eye on that child. There are bound to be deeply hidden emotional scars that some day will manifest themselves, possibly in some form of sociologically hostile tendencies."

Which are exactly the words his mother and I used after he left the room. For the next two years we watched him carefully. As nearly as we could tell, the only effects seemed to be that his grades improved, he became a starter on the football team and he turned out to be one of the most popular kids in school. He did, however, develop two zits on his forehead. Which may or may not call for therapy.

At the risk of adding more blemishes to his skin, I decide to tell him and his brother that I am getting married once more. I sit them down in the living room of my apartment.

"Guys, I have something to tell you. It's about me and . . . " Before I can finish my announcement, my middle son interrupts.

"I need a ride to Ray's house on Saturday night," he says.

"Well, we can talk about that later," I tell him. "Right now, I have some pretty important news. Your old dad's getting married again this summer."

There is a long moment of silence. Finally, he looks at me and says: "So, what's that got to do with me getting a ride to Ray's house?"

It takes a lot to get a kid's attention. But I do manage to get it with my next announcement. That's the one about the wedding date being the same day he was planning to leave for football camp.

While the subject of our impending marriage is of only passing interest to my kids, it causes considerably more reaction from her family, most of which I meet a few weeks later at her 13-year-old's *bar mitzvah.*

"This will be a wonderful opportunity for you to get to know my family," she tells me as we drive to the first of what will turn out to be 30 or 40 meals on the *bar mitzvah* weekend.

"I'm looking forward to it," I say.

We arrive at the restaurant where the dinner is to be served. The parking lot is packed.

"Must be a convention in town," I observe.

"No, we reserved the restaurant."

"You mean all these cars belong to your relatives?"

"These are just the ones from out of town."

Coming from a family in which reunions could have been held in the back seat of a DeSoto, I am not prepared to meet the stampede of aunts, uncles, nieces, nephews and cousins that thunders toward us as we walk through the door of the restaurant. Immediately we are surrounded by a reception committee of hugging and kissing relatives. Before I can get my coat off, I have been introduced to — and kissed on the cheek by — six aunts, four nieces and a remarkably friendly waiter.

While she disappears into a swarm of hugging and kissing cousins, I find a spot where I am not in danger of being trampled to death by a herd of blue-haired aunts. After a few minutes, an uncle approaches me.

"I understand you're marrying my niece," he says.

"Yes, sir, I am."

"*Mazel Tov,*" he says, sticking out his hand.

"It's very nice to meet you, Mr. Tov," I say, shaking his hand.

He gives me a funny look.

"You're not Jewish, are you," he says. It is not a question.

"No, sir, I'm not. How did you know?"

"Just a wild guess."

In the next 20 minutes I am approached by half a dozen more uncles, all of whom are named Tov. It is, apparently, a very popular Jewish name.

Eventually we sit down for dinner. The woman next to me is a cousin from New York.

"I hope you realize you're marrying a wonderful girl," she informs me.

Two possible replies enter my mind. The first is, "No, as a matter of fact I just assumed she was despicable pond-scum and if I'd known she was a wonderful girl I would have dumped her like last week's cat box filler." I decide to go with my second alternative.

"Yes, ma'am," I agree.

"You're going to be good to her, aren't you?"

Once again, there are two options. But I reject, "Actually, right after the honeymoon I had planned to take her home, chain her to the microwave and beat her three times a day."

I stick with, "Yes, ma'am."

Dinner ends. There is another flurry of hugging and kissing as everyone says goodbye before driving the five miles to the temple, where there will be more hugging and kissing when we see each other again.

After which there will be religious services and another round of goodbye hugs and kisses. Followed by a return trip to the restaurant for desserts, hugs and kisses.

"I hope you like my family," she says as we drive away from the restaurant.

I assure her that her family seems very nice and I am looking forward to joining it. I only hope my digestive system is up to it.

Not to mention my cheeks.

PREFACE: CHAPTER 2

# PROMISES

Our wedding will be a day of promise and promises.

In the presence of God, family and friends (not to mention a caterer, a harpist and a string quartet), we will repeat the customary promises to love and to honor, to be together in good times and in bad, in sickness and in health, until death us do part.

But we both have made those promises before and found them easier to say than to keep. And so there is another promise we need to make on the day we blend our families, a promise that may mean more than all the others.

It is a promise that we will try to remember the lessons we have learned from marriages past.

• That marriage really is a merger of equals and that the contract we are signing does not contain the terms "junior partner" or "minority shareholder." It was important, in their time, for our mothers to stand behind our fathers. It is important, in our time, for us to stand side-by-side.

• That there is no such thing in a marriage as "women's work" and "men's work." A steam iron, after all, is not a terribly complicated piece of machinery. My sons will not think less of me if they happen to see me iron my own shirt. Or even, their mother's blouse. Nor is it a threat to my manhood if she gets behind the wheel of the car and I sit in the passenger's seat.

• That there is no place either of us ever will be that is "too far" from a telephone if one of us doesn't know where the other one is. One thing living alone has taught us is that not having to check in with someone isn't simply "freedom." It also means that there is no one at home who cares.

• That her "need" to get a manicure is no less important than my "need" to play tennis. That sitting in front of a televised football game for three hours is no more a waste of time than talking on the phone for three hours.

• That there is no such thing as an innocent flirtation, a harmless deception or a casual affair. And that no matter how liberal and sophisticated we would like to think we have become, even a little bit of unfaithfulness is a poison without an antidote.

• That our children, no matter how much we love them, are not the reason for our marriage. How happy will they be with us if we don't make the time and effort to find happiness with each other?

• That our jobs, no matter how significant they may be to our egos, are not the reason for our lives. How important is it to make money "for us" if there is no "us"?

• That saying "please" and "thank you" always is proper, even in a marriage. Or, maybe, especially in a marriage.

• That saying "you look wonderful" always is appreciated.

• That saying "I'm sorry" is not a sign of weakness. Erich Segal was wrong when he told the world that love means never having to say you're sorry. When he wrote those words, he had not yet been married.

• That it is better to let the air out of little irritations by discussing them than to let them build up steam that can blow apart a relationship.

• That the details of our past loves are not nearly as fascinating to the other person as they are to us.

• That we are there not only to share our successes, but also our disappointments.

• That the need to hear "I love you" does not end with the honeymoon.

And on a day of promise and promises, the most important promise of all is that we will try to remember the feelings of love that have brought us to this day. If we can remember that, keeping the other promises will be easy.

# CHAPTER 2

The trouble with marriages is that too many of them start out with weddings. And having been down the aisle once before is not much help, because second weddings are different from first weddings.

First weddings are planned by the bride, the bride's mother, the bride's hair-stylist and every girlfriend the bride has had since second grade. When the last detail has been worked out, the groom gets a message on his answering machine telling him when to show up and what to wear.

Second marriages are a head-to-head confrontation.

The planning for our encores at the altar starts smoothly enough.

"I think we should have a wedding," I say.

"I agree," she says. It is not a phrase I will hear again.

"It probably shouldn't be anything too elaborate," I suggest. "We don't want your dad to have to spend a lot of money."

"What does my dad have to do with it?"

"The father of the bride always pays for the wedding."

"Not when it's the second wedding. I mean, I'm sure he'd be glad to pay for it if I asked him, but I'm not going to ask him."

"I suppose that means asking your ex-husband to pay for it is out of the question."

"We're going to have to pay for this one ourselves," she says.

"Well, then, we'd better limit the guest list."

"I've already trimmed mine," she says, reaching into her purse and pulling out a stack of papers thick enough to herniate Arnold Schwarzenegger.

"What's with the phone book?" I ask.

"It's not a phone book. It's a list of my friends that we absolutely cannot have the wedding without. The Sternbergs, the Weprins, the Szakals, the Kastans, the Leahys, the . . . "

"Who are the Leahys?"

"They're the best friends of the Goldmans. We can't invite the Goldmans without inviting the Leahys."

"Who are the Goldmans?"

"I told you about them. My 13-year-old went to their nephew's *bar mitzvah* three years ago."

"Have I ever met the Leahys?"

"*I've* never met the Leahys. But if we don't invite them, they'll never talk to us again."

"The last thing I want is for some people we've never met not to talk to us again. But, I'm warning you, if we invite all these people to the reception, it's going to cost us an awful lot of money for the beer."

"Beer? We can't serve beer with lobster-avocado mousse. The caterer wouldn't stand for it."

"What caterer?"

"The caterer who will be doing the food. Unless you were planning to have our guests brown bag it."

"Of course not. But don't you have some aunts who can make potato salad and some of those little roast beef sandwiches that taste like cardboard?"

"I'm not going to the trouble of renting chairs, tables and linen and having the florist custom-design the centerpieces and then serve potato salad and cardboard sandwiches."

"Why do we need all that stuff in the first place? Why can't we just serve the food on paper plates and let people stand around and eat?"

"Because," she sighs, "if everybody's milling around, no one will be able to hear the harpist."

"What harpist?"

"The harpist who is going to play when the string quartet is on its break. You *were* planning to have music at the reception, weren't you?"

"Sure. In fact, I've already contacted a buddy of mine who's a part-time disc jockey and he said he'd bring his entire collection of Little Richard records and . . . "

"Maybe we should talk about something else," she interrupts. "How about the honeymoon."

"I've taken care of that," I assure her. "I called the travel agent yesterday."

"Great. Where are we going?"

"It's a surprise. But it's a really neat place. Trust me."

"Of course I trust you. One of the things I love about you is that you're so romantic. Not like my friend Carol's husband. On their honeymoon he took her to Gatlinburg. Can you believe it? She said they stayed at a place called the Grits 'n Gravy Motel and spent all their time in souvenir shops that sold busts of Elvis carved out of corn cobs."

"The guy sounds like a real loser," I agree.

The next day I call my travel agent, cancel our reservations in the honeymoon suite at the Grits 'n Gravy Motel and make new plans.

"I changed my mind about the honeymoon trip," I tell my impending bride that evening. "The travel agent said it wasn't really a good choice this time of year because of all the commotion when Charles and Diana show up. So, instead, we're going to spend 10 days in New England. How does that sound?"

"Sounds wonderful," she says.

"It is. There's this picturesque little inn on the Cape you're going to love. And just a few miles down the road is a terrific restaurant we always enjoyed that serves the greatest clam chowder."

"We?"

"My first wife and I. We used to go there a lot. We'd drop the kids at her mother's and then we'd . . . "

"Let me see if I have the picture here," she cuts in. "You're proposing that we spend our honeymoon at a place where you used to make whoopie with your first wife?"

"Of course not. We hardly whoopied at all. Mostly we played tennis and sailed and went for walks in the woods. With all that exercise, we usually were too tired to whoopie."

"Gee, I'm sorry to hear that. Maybe if you called her and suggested that she meet us there, you and I could play doubles with her and her mother. And she might want to bring along the minister who performed your ceremony and . . . "

"Hey, wait a minute," I say, "you're not crazy about this New England idea, are you?"

"Don't be silly. What woman wouldn't love to go on her honeymoon to a hotel where the desk clerk calls the groom by his first name and the bellhop asks him if he wants breakfast at the usual time?"

"Okay, okay, I'll call my travel agent again and make different plans."

The next day I announce that a new itinerary has been drawn up for the honeymoon.

"We're going to spend a week in San Francisco," I inform her. "My travel agent said she thinks she can get us a good rate on a suite at the Fairmont Hotel."

"Try to get a suite facing west," she suggests. "They have a terrific view of the sunset on the Bay."

"You've been there before?"

"Sure. But I'd love to visit San Francisco again. When my ex and I were there, we didn't get to see many of the sites because we spent just about every minute in our room."

"Must have been a terrible trip," I agree. "Listen, how about if we find a place where neither of us has been before? I don't want this marriage to start off haunted by old memories."

"Good idea," she says, pulling an atlas out of the bookcase. After an hour of poring over maps, we have eliminated everything but North Dakota.

"What's your feeling on separate honeymoons?" she asks.

"It's probably not the best way to start a marriage," I point out. "Besides, I have an idea for a trip to some place I know neither one of us has been to before. Let me check with my travel agent again."

"Where is it?"

"I don't want to say until I get the details worked out. I want to surprise you."

*"PORTugal?!!!"*

Her voice ricochets through the terminal at New York's JFK airport, drowning out the roars of incoming 747s.

"We're going to *PORTugal?!!!!"*

I guess she is surprised.

OK, so maybe Portugal isn't the honeymoon destination of her dreams. Maybe, on a list of places where she had hoped to spend the first 10 days of our married life, it fell somewhere behind Baghdad, Nicaragua and the Bermuda Triangle.

But it hadn't been easy, finding a place that did not come encumbered with memories of previous marriages, specters of previous relationships. I had been to most of the countries in Europe. She had been to virtually every resort in the Western hemisphere where they served poolside pina coladas. So when a friend suggested that Portugal was a terrific alternative, it sounded perfect.

Not that my friend actually had been to Portugal. Nobody I talked to, in fact, ever had been to Portugal. Which only increased its attractiveness for me. If we went to Portugal and had a lousy time, we could come home and lie about it and no one would know the difference.

And my travel agent agreed that Portugal was a, uh, unique spot for a honeymoon.

"It's probably the best bargain in Europe right now," she had said. "And it's a lovely country."

"You enjoyed it?" I asked.

"I've never been there," she said.

On the strength of her endorsement, I booked two air/hotel packages and informed my bride-to-be that the honeymoon was all set.

"Where are we going?" she asked.

"I want it to be a surprise," I replied. "That'll make it more romantic."

Which is mostly the truth. Totally the truth is that I'm pretty sure if I tell her in advance that it's Portugal, the only ones standing under the ceremonial canopy on our wedding day will be me and the judge.

But she shows up for the wedding, we exchange our vows and now we are in the middle of the six-hour flight to Lisbon on TAP, the official Portuguese airline.

"Darling," she asks, when the stomach pains from our official Portuguese airline dinner have subsided.

"Yes, sweetheart?" I answer, stifling a belch. It is, after all, our honeymoon.

"What are we going to do in Portugal?"

I outline the itinerary that the travel agent has drawn up. We will spend the first five nights in Cascais, a picturesque fishing village just west of Lisbon. Then we will rent a car and drive to Evora, a picturesque Moorish city in the center of the country. Our last two nights will be in the Algarve, known throughout Europe as the Riviera of Portugal. And very picturesque.

"It sounds nice," she agrees. "But, what I meant was, what are we going to *do* there? I mean, if we were going to Paris, we could visit the Louvre and explore the Left Bank. If we were going to London, we could go to the theater and shop at Harrod's. What do visitors to Portugal do exactly, besides write sonnets?"

"There'll be plenty to do,"I assure her. "They have some beautiful old Catholic churches in Lisbon. And we can take a pilgrimage to the shrine of Fatima. And in Evora we're going to spend the night in an old restored convent."

"Wonderful," she says. "I can't wait to get home and show the snapshots to my rabbi."

It is early morning when we touch down at the Lisbon airport. A uniformed chauffeur drives us to our hotel in a Mercedes limousine. Like most of the people we will meet in the next 10 days, he speaks limited English. And, like most of the drivers we will see in the next 10 days, his secret ambition is to race at LeMans. Immediately we discover that cars in Portugal come in only two varieties: Those that are moving at 110 kilometers an hour and those that are parked with at least three wheels on the sidewalk.

Our hotel in Cascais is clean, semi-modern and run by a staff that can shrug its shoulders in a dozen languages. Shoulder shrugging in Portugal transcends the language barrier. Depending on the situation, it means, "I don't understand;" "I do understand, but I don't give a damn;" or "Yankee go home as soon as your wallet is empty." Not that shoulder shrugging is peculiar to Portugal. I also have encountered it in parts of Mexico, France, Italy, the Soviet Union, Poland, the Bahamas and most American discount stores.

The seaside town of Cascais is as scenic as a travel magazine feature. Boats bob on the water. Fishermen stand on the docks and repair their nets. Women walk topless along the beach.

At first, she is bothered by the semi-nudity.

"It's nothing to be shocked about," I say, glancing in her direction from time to time. "It's just a different way of life here. People in Europe don't have the silly sexual hangups that we do. They realize that the human body is nothing to be ashamed of."

"When you put it that way, I suppose you're right," she says, reaching for the clasp of her bathing suit.

"Are you crazy?" I shout, throwing my beach mat over her. "You're my wife."

On our third evening I convince her to go to a bullfight. She is reluctant, because she doesn't want to see an animal suffer. If a fly came into our living room, she wouldn't swat it, she would reason with it. But I explain to her that in Portugal the matadors don't kill the bull. They merely run around in tight pants for a while and annoy it. When the fight is over, the bull is taken away, uninjured. Then somebody else kills it.

The bull, we discover at our first Portuguese bullfight, is not the dumbest animal in the ring. Portuguese bullfights also include eight unarmed, unpadded men who stand in the ring in single file. The man in front shouts insults at the bull. When the bull has heard enough, he lowers his head and charges. The man in front jumps on the bull's head, preferably between his horns. (I am not making this up.) Then the other seven men grab whatever part of the bull is handy and attempt to subdue it. We had never seen anything like it. Except for the time eight midget wrestlers took on Andre the Giant.

But we have not come to Portugal just for culture. We also have come to relax. So mostly we spend our five days in Cascais swimming, sunbathing, shopping and exploring the many mysteries of the country. One of the many mysteries of the country is how a restaurant surrounded on three sides by the Atlantic Ocean could charge prices for a piece of fish that would make the maitre d' at Lutece blush.

Other meals, however, are bargains. A good pork dinner, including a bottle of green house wine, seldom costs more than 1,500 *escudos.* At the official exchange rate of 147 *escudos* to the dollar, that comes to about $12. Or $120. We never do quite get the hang of it.

We eat frequently and well. Potatoes are the best we ever have tasted. Gazpacho is great. Beer and wine are cheap. And virtually every restaurant offers *frango,* which is spring chicken, marinated and grilled. The Colonel's chicken, in comparison, tastes like fried buzzard.

But he, or she, who *frangos* too often eventually pays the price.

On the fourth morning of our honeymoon she awakens with Columbus' revenge. I go to the supermarket in search of Pepto-Bismol. The supermarket sells groceries, hardware, stereos, washing machines and automobiles. But no medicine. Medicine can be purchased only at the *farmacia*. I go to the *farmacia*. There is no Pepto-Bismol on the shelves. I thumb through my phrase book.

*"Minha mulher esta doente,"* I tell the man behind the counter. Which, with any luck, means "my wife is ill." While the customers behind me watch, I clutch my midsection to make it clear that my *mulher's* illness is an upset stomach. I put my hand on my forehead to indicate that it also involves a headache. I am aware that another part of her problem is diarrhea. But there are only so many pantomimes I am willing to do in public, even for a new *mulher.*

On the fifth day she has recovered sufficiently to leave the bathroom. I arrange to have a rental car brought to the hotel. It is a white Austin Mini.

"What's this?" she demands when she sees it.

"It's our rental car. What does it look like?"

"It looks like a refrigerator."

The Mini, it turns out, also handles like a refrigerator. Because the car is so small, obviously some of the options had to be left out. Among the options left out were springs and shock absorbers.

We drive north over scenic Portuguese roads, many of which have been paved in this century. After three hours we bounce into Fatima where, on May 13, 1917, three young shepherds reported the appearance of the Virgin Mary. On the 13th of every month since then, thousands of pilgrims make the trip to the site, many of them covering the last hundred yards on their knees. Several miracles have been attributed to the shrine.

We park our car and join the pilgrims inside the church. When we return to our car we are disappointed to see that the miracle for which we have prayed has not happened. The Austin Mini has not turned into a BMW.

From Fatima we drive to Evora, where we have a rented room in a *pousada.* Operated by the government, *pousadas* are scattered throughout Portugal and frequently are located in restored castles or historic monasteries. This particular *pousada* is located in the Convent of Loios, which dates from the 16th Century. The *pousada* is charming, we agree, but it feels strange, honeymooning in a convent. That night, we both have headaches.

The next day we drive to the Algarve, 200 miles south of Lisbon. The Algarve is popular as a resort area, which means hotels are newer, shops are more chic and a Sagres beer that costs 100 *escudos* in Evora runs 350 *escudos*. Which is somewhere between $4 and $600, American.

But on our last night in Portugal, we decide to splurge. We make reservations in a fancy restaurant in a five-star hotel. I order a bottle of Dom Perignon. We have entrees flambeed at tableside. When the bill comes, it is 32,000 *escudos.* It takes several seconds for my heart to resume beating. I still have no idea exactly how much that is, but 32,000 anythings on a tab tends to alter your rhythm for a while.

The next day we fly home, relaxed, yet tired. We are, after all, no *frangos* anymore. Still, it has been a terrific honeymoon. She is pleased. I am relieved. Portugal has been a pleasant surprise for both of us.

But now it is time to get on to some serious family blending.

# HOW IS MARRIED LIFE?

In the first few weeks after the wedding, the toughest part about being married is responding to people who ask:

"How's married life?"

I never quite know how to reply.

Just to see the expression on people's faces, the temptation is strong to say, "Married life is a living hell that not even Dante could have imagined if he'd had a bowl of bad peyote for breakfast."

But I don't say that, because it's not true, necessarily.

On the other hand, I could tell them that "married life is a state of unadulterated bliss too exquisite to describe."

I don't say that, either. Because people who know me are aware that I tend not to get carried away like that. If I came back from a 10-day business trip to heaven, the most I would say about the place was that it was "nice."

Besides, people who ask "How's married life?" are just making polite conversation and really aren't all that interested, any more than they really want to know, "How's it going?", "What's new?" or "Is it cold enough for you?"

So, generally, I just say "fine" and they say "that's great" and the conversation turns to more urgent subjects, like football.

Which probably is just as well. Because there doesn't seem to be a short answer to a question as complicated as "How's married life?" Marriage brings with it a whole world of changes.

Some of the changes merely are clerical: Names, addresses, phone numbers, insurance policies.

Some are physical: Medicine cabinets must be shared. Blouses have to be scrunched together a little closer to make room for dress shirts. A few Evian bottles and yogurt cartons may have to move over in the refrigerator to make room for a six-pack and a bottle of hot salsa.

Other changes run deeper: Options for one become decisions for two. New living room furniture must satisfy her tastes and his size. The next car may be less than his dream but more than her wish. A vacation trip no longer is simply a matter of arranging one work schedule.

And sometimes the changes happen so subtly that they are not immediately apparent: No matter how long you have dated and/or lived together, premarital plans seem to have an unspoken asterisk after them. There is always that possibility, however small, that the marriage might never happen and that it is pointless to talk about what might take place 10 years from now. But the wedding ceremony is a spoken commitment to long-range planning.

If married life changes the way you look at the world, it also changes the way the world looks at you. Especially if you're a man.

The world tends to ask questions, and draw conclusions, about a man who never has been married. He is immature. He is self-centered. He is unable to make a commitment. And he is, if he is over 40, probably gay. That's how the world tends to think.

It asks questions and draws conclusions, too, about a man who is divorced. He is flawed. He is unable to sustain a relationship. He probably drinks, gambles and runs around. Even in this most enlightened of all possible times, the question most often asked in the wake of a divorce is, "What did *he* do?"

But marriage, or re-marriage, brings with it the stamp of stability in the world's eyes. A man who marries has conformed. He has been civilized. Children are safer around him. Whatever the reality, a man who wears a wedding band is perceived as more likely to pay his bills, drive sensibly and wear clean underwear. Less likely to wake up some Monday morning with a hangover, quit his job and run off to Club Med to carouse his life away.

There are, I'm sure, a lot of changes yet to come as a result of this marriage and it's possible that there never will be a simple answer to the question, "How's married life?" Except, of course, that it is "different."

# CHAPTER 3

○○○

The greatest challenges facing a man when he remarries, most experts will tell you, have to do with adjusting to her kids, her ex-husband, her friends, sex, money and the position of the toilet seat.

In my case, the experts aren't even close. In the early days of our wedded bliss, the greatest challenge I face is trying to figure out where the heck she keeps the colander.

The problem is that, like many men, I have a tendency to arrange things systematically. In three years of bachelorhood, my spices were lined up alphabetically in the spice rack. My soup cans were stacked together. My baking supplies were clustered in the cupboard. If I accidentally wound up with more than one bottle of catsup, the newest one was pushed to the back of a shelf and was not eligible to move into the refrigerator until the first bottle was empty.

It's different in her kitchen, I quickly learn.

Not only is her spice rack not arranged alphabetically, she does not own a spice rack. Parsley usually hides behind the flour, sage may or may not be next to the spray starch, rosemary is under the sink and the last time I saw thyme it was in the junk drawer with a pair of scissors, three empty bottles of Elmer's glue, the 10-year-old's penny collection, 12 pounds of sheet metal screws and a tennis ball that had turned green.

Soup cans are likely to be found behind any cupboard door you dare to open in her kitchen. And several in the living room. There are, I suspect, enough ingredients in our condo to bake a cake the size of the Kremlin. But it would take the KGB to find them all.

In all fairness, she doesn't get much help from her kids, who will eat a

Popsicle and put the stick back into the freezer.

None of which would matter much, except that I happen to enjoy cooking occasionally. Two days after we return from the honeymoon, for instance, I volunteer to prepare a spaghetti dinner while she catches up on some work she has brought home.

To start, I fill a large pot with water and put it on the stove. When the spaghetti is in the pot I assemble a salad of lettuce (last used by the 10-year-old, who accidentally returned it to the refrigerator), onions (in a basket under the telephone), garlic (in the garlic cellar on top of the answering machine), tomato (on the window sill) and black olives (on a shelf, between the cat food and the leftover invitations to the 13-year-old's *bar mitzvah*. Which was last April).

"Sweetheart?" I ask when the salad is assembled.

"Yes, my darling?" says a voice from the living room.

"What kind of dressing would you like on your salad?"

"What kind do we have?"

"Well, in the refrigerator we have three half-empty bottles of creamy Italian, four unopened bottles of Russian, a completely empty bottle of Thousand Island and an industrial-size jar of mayonnaise with a spoon growing out of it. In the pantry we have two bottles of Dijon vinaigrette and something with Paul Newman's picture on it. In the liquor cabinet we have . . . "

"All right, all right, I get the picture. I'll have Italian . . . dear."

"Fine . . . honey."

I check the spaghetti. It is perfectly *al dente.* I turn off the burner and look for the colander. It is not in the pantry. It is not in the cupboard. It is not in the oven, the refrigerator, the microwave, the toaster or the Cuisinart. By now the spaghetti is *al soggy.*

"Hey," I shout.

"Now what?"

"Where's the colander?"

"Right where it always is. In the upstairs linen closet."

I am tempted to endanger our wedded bliss by pointing out that storing the colander in the upstairs linen closet is just about the most illogical thing I have ever heard. But I stop myself just in time. If I have learned one thing about marriage, it is that there is no room in it for logic.

Besides, deciding where the colander should live is just one of approximately four billion things that have to be worked out when two people try to share the same space. But, having both been there before, we thought we had anticipated most of the big ones.

Long before the wedding, we discussed finances, religion and politics. We drew up schedules that covered everything from vacations to bathroom time. We decided who would shop and who would cook, who would wash and who would dry, who would bring in the mail and who

would put out the cat. We even touched on who was entitled to at least one night out a week with the girls and what would happen to him if he ever tried it.

After months of negotiations, we walked down the aisle secure in the belief that this would be a battle-free relationship. Somehow, we both forgot about the closet wars.

I don't care what the marriage counselors say, more divorces start in clothes closets than in singles bars, swingers' clubs or $29.95 motel rooms. The problem is particularly acute in second marriages. After a few years of bachelorhood, a man gets used to being able to reach his bowling shirt without having to fight his way past Liz Claiborne, Anne Klein and Yves St. Laurent.

The problem in our closet is not immediately apparent when I move from my apartment to her condo and bring along my wardrobe. Half of which I am wearing at the time.

"Which side of the closet would you like, my darling?" she sighs.

"I wouldn't dream of displacing any of your clothes, my angel," I murmur. "I'll just hang my stuff on a doorknob."

"Don't be silly, my precious," she coos. "I'd rather douse a Coco Chanel original with lighter fluid and set fire to it than have my clothes take up your space in the closet."

The issue is settled. She and Coco will occupy the left side of the closet. Levi and I will hang out on the right side. The arrangement is perfect. For about a week.

Which is when I walk to my half of the closet and find a Donna Karan blouse and a Bill Blass skirt hanging between my Joe Namath sport coat and my Sans-A-Belt slacks. I check the tag in back of the skirt. It is a size 4. As I suspected, the skirt is not mine.

"Dear?" I call.

"Yes, honey?" comes the answer.

"Why are there a skirt and a blouse hanging in my side of the closet?"

"They just came back from the dry cleaner's and I didn't have room for them on my side. You don't mind, do you? They're only taking up a little bit of your space."

"Well, I guess it's all right."

It is the first mistake of my second marriage. My border has been crossed. The occupation of my closet territory has begun.

Sometime that night, the Donna Karan blouse and the Bill Blass skirt get together and reproduce seven dresses, 16 sweaters, 28 pairs of shoes, a flimsy peignoir I haven't seen since the honeymoon and a flannel bathrobe I've seen a lot of lately. All of which wind up on my side of the closet.

When the invasion reaches a point where the only thing I can squeeze into my side of the closet is a sock, I decide to bring it to her attention.

"Hey, buster," I bellow.

"Now what?"

"Is it asking too much for you to keep the MGM wardrobe department on your side of the closet?"

"I hope you're not referring to the few pitiful items of clothing I own. I know nudists who have a more extensive wardrobe than I do. There are peasants in China who have more clothes. There are bag ladies in Manhattan who . . . "

When she gets to the part about how there are nuns in convents with a larger collection of cocktail dresses than she has, I tune her out. I have fought this war before and I still am paying reparations.

Besides, she did say I was welcome to hang my clothes on any doorknob I liked.

Who hangs what where is just one of the issues that makes second marriages a little more complicated than first marriages. First marriages are fresh slates. Second marriages start on a blackboard scribbled with unbreakable habits, entrenched routines and non-negotiable differences.

Setting up housekeeping, for instance, was a relatively simple matter the first time I got married. She had towels in her hope chest. I had my grandmother's old green over-stuffed sofa. Some friends bought us a vinyl-topped card table. We put them all together and had enough room left in our apartment to hold the Democratic National Convention.

This time it's a little more complicated. Between us, we have two past marriages, six kids and nearly 40 years' worth of accumulated stuff. She has a condo full of furniture. I have an apartment full of furniture. And, if we try to put them all together, our place is going to look like an Ethan Allen warehouse. It's obvious that compromises are going to be necessary.

Some of them are easy. With hardly any debate, we agree that we will keep her Henredon country French dining room set and get rid of my vinyl-topped card table. She also makes a strong case for keeping her bedroom set instead of mine, even though the top of my dresser only recently has been covered with fresh contact paper.

It's when we get to the living room that the problems begin.

"I think it makes more sense to keep my living room furniture," she says.

"Why?"

"For one thing, my couch and chairs are practically brand new and they're good quality and very expensive."

"That could be. But I happen to think my living room furniture has more character than yours."

"I don't want to start off this marriage with furniture you bought by mail," she declares. "Besides, my furniture coordinates better with the artwork."

"What artwork?"

"Well, there's the print hanging over my fireplace, for instance."

"You mean that thing with the red and orange blobs of paint? You're not serious. Don't get me wrong, I think it's nice that you're proud of your 10-year-old's artwork, but most people usually tape stuff like that on the refrigerator door next to the Family Circus cartoons and the Ann Landers columns."

"For your information, that happens to be a very valuable print. It was signed and numbered by the artist."

"I don't care if Van Gogh personally came to your house and cut off his ear in the living room while he was painting it. It looks like something you'd buy at an abandoned gas station after all the glow-in-the-dark Elvis portraits were gone."

"Fine," she sniffs. "Then what exactly do you suggest we hang in the living room, your *Playboy* centerfold collection?"

"As a matter of fact, I was thinking that the framed poster I bought when I was at Mardi Gras a few years ago would look terrific over the fireplace."

"Just what every family's living room needs, a bright red portrait of a New Orleans transvestite. I'd rather look at Miss December."

Eventually, we decide to keep her living room furniture and put mine in storage until we find a house big enough to hold it all. And we reach a compromise on the artwork question, too.

We're going to keep all of her prints. But we're going to hang them on my nails.

Even if we had decided to keep some of my artwork, there wouldn't be any place to put them. The condo already is lousy with decorations, all of which are part of what is known as "a woman's touch."

As nearly as I can tell, "a woman's touch" involves seeing how many pieces of non-functional clutter can be stuffed into one room before the floor begins to sag in the middle and the foundation suffers structural damage.

During my bachelor period, I didn't give a great deal of thought to interior decorating. The way I figured it, drapes on the windows and a Bernie Kosar poster on the wall were enough decoration for any room. But as soon as I become a non-bachelor again, my world is crammed with candles that never will be lighted, crystal bowls that never will contain nacho chips and bookcases in which there is no room for books.

And baskets.

Our condo is a basket warehouse. Baskets sit on our floors and roost on our shelves. They hang on our walls and dangle in front of our windows. They lurk in our closets and clone in our cupboards. Our condo looks like a cruise ship stop in the Bahamas.

All of which might not bother me if the woman who bought them doesn't start campaigning for a new house the day after I move in.

"This place is too small for all of us," she announces. "There's no room to put anything."

"There'd be enough room to hold the Winter Olympics if you'd clear out some of the junk in here," I point out.

"What, exactly, do you mean by 'junk?' "

"Junk is anything you can't cook in, eat off or drink out of."

"Fine. Then let's get rid of your tennis racquets."

"I was thinking about some of these baskets."

"What are you talking about? I'm not throwing away any of those baskets. We need them."

"Are you kidding? The Easter Bunny doesn't need this many baskets. What good are they?"

"They're the 'in' accessory."

"Says who?"

"My interior decorator. He's helped most of my friends furnish their places and he's recommended that they all decorate with a lot of baskets, too."

"Of course he has. I'll bet interior decorating is only a sideline with him. He's probably really making his money as a basket manufacturer. My guess is that he has a family of illegal aliens turning them out in his basement for starvation wages and . . . "

"Don't be ridiculous," she says. "Anyway, these baskets are very functional."

"Functional? So far the only function I've seen them perform is to fall off the top of the refrigerator every time I open the door."

"They're perfect for entertaining," she counters. "You can fill them with crackers and fruit. Or you can use them to hold flowers. If you have people over for dinner, you can set them on the table with bread or hot rolls."

"How are we ever going to have people over for dinner? The dining room is so full of baskets they'd have to eat in the driveway."

"I've asked you a million times not to exaggerate," she says. "I really don't have that many."

She's right, I guess. She really doesn't have that many baskets. Not compared with how many house plants she has.

To be fair about it, I suspected that she was a house plant addict before I married her. I suspected it, in fact, on our first date when I went to pick her up at her condo and she handed me a machete at the door and told me to hack my way to the couch.

"So," I said, after I had fought my way past a particularly aggressive Boston fern, "who does your decorating . . . Luther Burbank?"

"Why do you ask?"

"I don't know. It's just that you seem to have a lot of things growing in here. Do the other guys you date wear loincloths and hang around with chimpanzees a lot?"

"It's just that I love house plants," she explained. "Don't you?"

"Of course," I agreed. "I don't think I could live in a place that didn't have house plants." (Which was not the truth, exactly. The truth, exactly, was that I would have had no trouble spending the rest of my life in a place where the only green things in sight were Rolling Rock beer bottles. But when you are on a first date, you will agree with her if she says she loves acid rain, oil spills and nuclear accidents. Especially when it's been four months since your last date.)

"Do you have a lot of plants in your apartment?" she asked.

"Well, no, not a lot," I admitted. (Which was not the truth, exactly, either. The truth, exactly, is that in three years of singlehood I purchased approximately six house plants — only one of which survived the drive home from the discount store. That was the plant that lived for three months, until the weekend I was out of town and the 19-year-old's band practiced at our apartment. There is some confusion as to how the plant actually died. The 19-year-old swears that the lead singer ate it. I'm betting that the drummer smoked it).

Despite our early horticultural differences, the seeds of our love are planted, germinate and blossom into matrimony. And, on the way home from the honeymoon, we stop at the nursery to buy a potted *calceolaria* for the living room. The *calceolaria* is followed by a *sansevieria.* Which leads to a *schefflera.* Which has to be moved to make room for a trio of *rhipsalidopsis.* All of which take up so much room in our living room that I no longer can see our Mitsubishi.

Each day she spends two hours watering and fertilizing. Which is an hour and 50 minutes more than she spends making dinner. After six weeks of marriage, our vine-covered condo has become a greenhouse, a fact I decide to bring to her attention one day when she asks if I have seen the 10-year-old.

"Not see Boy," I grunt. "Maybe ask Cheetah."

"OK," she sighs, "out with it. Just what are you trying to say?"

"What I'm trying to say is that it's a jungle in here. This place isn't a home, it's a terrarium."

"You said you liked plants."

"I do. I think every house should have one. But you're getting a little carried away here. There are successful farmers in Iowa who don't have as many things growing as you do."

"Plants make the room bright and cheerful," she points out.

"Sunshine would make the room bright and cheerful, too. But I haven't seen the sun in here since the rehearsal dinner because every window in the place has a bunch of stupid house plants sitting in front of it."

"Shh," she says. "They'll hear you and sense your hostility."

"Hostility? What hostility? Just because the patio is covered with sphagnum moss, the kitchen cannisters are filled with vermiculite and I have to swing on three vines to get through the living room, why should I be hostile?"

"If I'd known you were a plant hater, I never would have married you," she sniffles. We are on the verge of our first major marital crisis.

"I don't hate plants," I say, doing my best to nip it in the bud.

"You don't?"

"Of course not," I assure her. "If I hadn't found you, I probably would have married a hibiscus. I'm sorry you got the wrong impression and I'm sorry I upset you. To make up for it, I'm going to stay home from work tomorrow and clean the condo."

"You are?"

"Yeah."

"That's so sweet."

I think I'll start by defoliating the living room.

# STEPDADS

If we can set aside one day each June to pay tribute to our fathers, what should we designate to honor the estimated 13 million American men who are stepfathers?

How about a week?

I don't mean to take anything away from the men whose careers as fathers started at the moment of conception. Fatherhood can be a tough and frequently thankless job and they deserve every hand-drawn card and Play-Doh ashtray they receive. But their job, no matter how tough and thankless, is a day on the golf course compared with the challenges that face many stepfathers.

Stepfathers are the relief pitchers of family life, substitutes brought in with the bases loaded and the opposing team running wild. They are second-string parents, bench warmers who weren't around at the beginning of the game when the rules were being made.

To a bachelor who never has played the game before, it may seem that there are no rules at all. Small boys race into their lives, shouting and pillaging. Teen-age girls burst into tears at the dinner table for no apparent reason.

No one forces men into stepfatherhood, of course. But it's virtually impossible to tell that the woman who catches your eye in the soft light of a cocktail lounge has a daughter at home whose idol is Madonna and a son whose ambition is to grow up to be Conan the Barbarian.

Without warning or adequate preparation, a relationship that started with candlelight and wine coolers suddenly turns into a world of blaring televisions and spilled milk. Annual trips to Club Med are replaced by death marches through Disneyworld. The Porsche gets traded in for a station wagon. The hands that mixed Bloody Marys now are expected to fix bicycles, string kites and reach down into the cold toilet water to rescue GI Joe. When the phone rings, it will not be a buddy suggesting you get together for tennis or a sweet young thing suggesting you get together for a drink. When the phone rings, it will not be for you.

With all that, the problems faced by men who jump directly from bachelorhood to stepfatherhood are not necessarily as complicated as those confronting men who bring a little bit of experience into the game.

Men enrolling into second families tend to think their kids are the standard model and that other kids differ only in size and shape. What they discover, frequently too late, is that the differences run deeper than mere packaging. Children are a product of the rules by which they are raised. And each family's rules are different.

For a man accustomed to meals eaten in the dining room to the sound of family conversation, it can be tough to swallow dinner in the living room to the sound of *Jeopardy.* A man who has raised kids trained never to interrupt an adult's conversation can have trouble adjusting to a kid who has been encouraged to jump in whenever something occurs to him.

What is a capital offense for his kids may be no more than a misdemeanor to hers. It's not that one way is right and the other is wrong. It's just that they are not the same.

"A second marriage is a different kind of battleground," a shell-shocked stepfather told me once.

No matter what a stepfather's previous experience, discipline eventually can become the field of screams in which there are no survivors. No matter how much a stepfather is tempted to lose his temper and let a kid know he's gone too far, it is difficult to yell at another man's child. No matter how much he thinks that all the kid needs to straighten him out is a good smack on the butt, it is dangerous to hit another man's child.

And a stepfather never totally forgets that he is living with another man's child. Because invariably, inevitably, he will hear:

"You're not my real father."

Still, there are rewards for the relief pitchers of family life. In his book, *Stepfathering,* author Mark Bruce Rosin quotes a man who points out the difference between being a stepfather and being a "real" father:

"We love each other because we want to, not because we are supposed to," the stepfather said. "With biological children, there is no choice."

A man who can think like that deserves at least a week in his honor.

Maybe a month.

# CHAPTER 4

OOOO

It isn't easy, being a wicked stepfather.

There are no guidelines. Western literature is filled with tips on how to become a wicked stepmother. Give your stepkid a poison apple. Make her clean the chimney while your daughters go to the ball. Ditch them in a forest and make them find their way home with bread crumbs.

Stepfathers don't get an instruction manual. They have to learn to be wicked on their own.

All I can do is my best.

When I arrived on the scene, I immediately forced my stepsons to:

- Knock on closed doors.
- Go to bed before David Letterman's stupid pet tricks.
- Flush.

Other changes, though, have to be approached cautiously and diplomatically. There is, for instance, the problem my wife and I encounter in our bedroom.

(I could have phrased that differently, I suppose. But I couldn't resist the temptation to put it in those words, just so I could see the look on her face when she gets to this page.)

Anyway, it's not that kind of problem. The problem has to do with kids and it starts the day after we come home from the honeymoon.

It is morning. She is getting ready to go back to work. I am curled up under the covers, working on another 40,000 winks. My attempt to get back to sleep is disrupted by the sound of voices. I open one eye. Our bedroom appears to be filled with vaguely familiar boys. I close my eye, pull a pillow over my head and return to what I was doing.

That evening I mention the incident to my wife.

"I had the strangest dream this morning," I tell her. "I dreamt that there was a Boy Scout den meeting in our bedroom."

"That wasn't a dream," she informs me. "My boys were in there getting ready for school."

"You let your kids come into our bedroom?"

"You have a problem with that?"

"Well, yes, I do. I think they're a little old to be coming into our bedroom unless there's a special reason."

"I suppose you're right," she agrees. "They aren't little boys anymore. It's probably not a good idea for them to be coming in while I'm getting dressed."

"Who's talking about you? I don't want them coming in while *I'm* getting dressed. Seeing a strange man in Jockey shorts and black socks is no way for a kid to start his day."

"Well, I guess we could talk to them about it."

That night we talk to them about it. We handle the subject frankly and honestly, explaining that the only reason they can't come in is because the fire marshal has declared that the maximum safe occupancy of our room is two persons. They promise they will stay out of our bedroom unless there is a special reason to enter it.

The next morning the 13-year-old walks into our bedroom at 6:32.

"Did you forget our conversation already?" I ask him.

"You said we could come in if there was a special reason," he says. "I need to borrow some hair spray."

He borrows the hair spray and leaves. At 6:36, the 10-year-old comes in.

"Why are you in here?" I inquire.

"Special reason," he says, heading for our bathroom. "I need some mousse." He mousses and leaves.

At 6:39 the 13-year-old returns.

"What is it now?" I demand. "Eye shadow?"

"Contact lens solution."

On the way out, he passes the 10-year-old, who is coming back to borrow some dental floss.

In half an hour they find 43 special reasons to come into our bedroom, the carpet between the door and our bathroom is starting to shine and the only thing in our medicine chest they haven't borrowed is the Midol.

For the next three mornings our bedroom continues to have more boys walking through it than a video game arcade. The only way I am going to be able to keep them out, I decide finally, is to strike a little fear into their hearts. The time for caution and diplomacy is over. I hate to do it, but I've got to be tough.

I'm going to have to let them see me in my Jockey shorts and black socks.

But my first chance to be really wicked is when I get into the shoe business.

My stepsons have this thing about shoes. When they enter the house, they do not take off their shoes and put them away. They merely walk out of them and leave them in the middle of the living room floor.

"Why do they do that?" I ask their mother one day.

"Do what?" she replies, kicking off her Reeboks and pushing them under the television.

"Leave their shoes in the middle of the living room."

"I guess it's just a habit I let them get into when I was single," she admits. "I tried to get them to put them away, but I just didn't have the energy. Nagging is a two-parent job."

"Well, things are going to change now that I'm around here," I promise.

That afternoon they come home from school, walk out of their shoes and head toward the refrigerator.

"Hold it, you guys," I say. "Do you see something wrong with those shoes?"

"Yeah, mine have holes in them," says the 13-year-old. "When can we buy some new ones?"

"That's not what I meant. I meant, don't you think there's something wrong with where you left them?"

"That's where we always leave them," he says. "Mom doesn't care."

"Well, I do. From now on, keep them on your feet or in your bedroom."

"Why?"

"Because I refuse to live in a house that looks like the entrance to a Japanese restaurant. Empty shoes don't belong in the living room. I was never allowed to leave my shoes in the living room when I was a kid."

"You told us you never had shoes when you were a kid," the 10-year-old says. "You said you were so poor you had to wrap your feet in borrowed newspapers and walk 12 miles through the snow to . . . "

"Never mind what I told you," I interrupt. "Do what I tell you."

The next day they both leave their shoes in the living room again. Apparently, sterner measures are needed to get their attention. That night, after they go to bed, I pick up their shoes, open the front door and throw them out into the front yard. Chuckling wickedly, I go to bed.

The next thing I know, there is a voice in my ear.

"Shoes," the voice is saying.

I open one eye. The clock says it is 7:15 a.m. I open the other eye to get a second opinion. The clock still says it is 7:15.

"The kids can't find their shoes," the owner of the voice says. "They're going to be late for school."

"I threw them out into the front yard," I mumble.

"Why in the world would you do that?"

"Because they don't belong in the living room."

"Let me see if I have this straight. They don't belong in the living room, but they *do* belong in the front yard? That doesn't make sense."

"I'll explain it later," I mutter, rolling over and fighting to get back to sleep. If she wanted sense at 7:15 in the morning, she should have married Bryant Gumbel. Besides, I'm not sure I can explain it to her. All I know is that it is important for me, as a stepfather, to establish who's in charge before they get big enough to throw my shoes out into the front yard.

With me in them.

The shoe showdown lasts for the next several weeks as her sons test me to see just how serious I am about this thing.

The problem is, I really don't know.

Even though I have been an accomplice to the raising of four kids of my own, stepfatherhood is so much different than fatherhood.

Fatherhood is immediate and absolute. One day you're not a father, the next day you are. One day you're strolling along the beach soaking up the sun and the next thing you know a giant wave has dragged you into an ocean of lumpy diapers, 4 a.m. feedings and ear infections. Just like that, it's sink or swim. You don't have time to think about whether it's better to dog paddle or backstroke. You just do what you can to keep your head above water.

Stepfatherhood is more like an icy lake. It's something you have to ease yourself into a little bit at a time. If you jump in head first, your system will never survive the shock.

For the first few months, I stand on the edge of stepfatherhood, only occasionally working up the nerve to dip a toe into the new waters. I am aware that a second marriage can be a tricky situation and that it is an especially difficult adjustment for teen-age boys whose mother has changed horses in midstream, so to speak.

But, eventually, circumstances force me to take the plunge.

The specific circumstance is that I am unable to locate my tennis racquet, which the 13-year-old borrowed shortly after the wedding and failed to return. I go up to his bedroom to look for it.

One glance tells me that, even if my racquet is in there, I'm never going to be able to find it under the pile of clothes, magazines, cassettes and composting bath towels covering the floor. Ivan Lendl could be in there and I'd never be able to find him.

I mention the subject to his mother.

"Have you looked in the 13-year-old's bedroom lately?" I inquire.

"He *has* left things sort of cluttered," she says.

"Hurricanes leave things sort of cluttered. That bedroom would qualify for federal disaster relief. You're going to have to say something to him about it."

"I've been saying something to him about it for five years," she sighs.

"He always promises to clean it up, but he never gets around to it. Maybe you'd have better luck."

When the 13-year-old gets home from school that afternoon, I sit him down in the living room.

"There seems to be a problem with your bedroom," I begin.

"You're absolutely right," he agrees. This is not going to be nearly as difficult as I thought.

"Well, then, what are we going to do about it?"

"I was thinking maybe you could drive me up to Radio Shack today. They're having a really good sale on . . . "

"Wait a minute. We're talking about the problem in your bedroom."

"So am I. The problem in my bedroom is that it doesn't have a CD player."

"How do you know?" I counter.

The 13-year-old thinks about that for a moment.

"You're trying to tell me something, aren't you?" he asks.

"I'm trying to tell you that your bedroom is a mess and I want it cleaned up right now. No excuses and no delays. The vacuum cleaner is in the hall closet. Take it up to your room and get to work."

Obviously impressed by my no-nonsense approach, he gets off the couch, takes the vacuum cleaner out of the hall closet and carries it upstairs. A minute later I hear the sound of the sweeper in his bedroom. Two minutes later I hear the sound of him carrying it back downstairs.

"What's the problem?" I ask.

"No problem. I'm done."

I am not one to doubt the word of a 13-year-old. On the other hand, I find it difficult to believe that five years' worth of disaster has been repaired that quickly. We walk upstairs to his bedroom together to inspect the clean-up effort. To the casual observer, there seems to be no difference in the depth of trash on his floor.

There can be only one explanation.

He vacuumed over it.

"I hate to be a nit-picker," I say. "But what I had in mind was for you to pick up all this stuff on the floor and *then* vacuum."

Three hours later he comes back downstairs to report that his bedroom is clean. I check it out. All the stuff that was in the middle of the floor has disappeared. I'm not sure what he has done with it, but I can't help noticing that the legs of his bed no longer touch the floor.

I decide not to press the issue. You can't be too fussy when you're up to your neck in the icy waters of stepfatherhood.

But as long as I am already all wet, I decide to head for the deep water.

I will swim over to the 10-year-old's room.

If the 13-year-old's room is messy, the 10-year-old's room is Squalor Valley. They could gather up the 160 million tons of garbage produced in the United States each year and dump it in the 10-year-old's room. He'd never notice.

It's not a bedroom, it's an unlicensed landfill. Carl Sagan can talk all he wants about the greenhouse effect. One look at this kid's room and he'll be talking about the outhouse effect.

It's not as if I haven't tried to get him to clean it. Cleaning his room, in fact, is just about the only thing we have talked about since I enlisted in this family. But he always has an excuse. In the morning, he is late for school. After school, he has homework to do. Before dinner, he is too hungry. After dinner, he is too full. At all other times he has to go to the bathroom first.

The only good thing about it all is that I don't have to nag him about making his bed. His bed disappeared under a pile of ripe underwear when he was seven.

But, fired up as a result of my semi-success with the 13-year-old, I give it another try.

"If I quit smoking, cut down on cholesterol and jog six hours a day, do you think I'll live long enough to see the 10-year-old clean up his room?" I ask his mother one afternoon.

"He promised he was going to clean it up last week," she replies.

"So, why didn't he?"

"I'm not sure. Maybe he couldn't figure out how to get a bulldozer up the stairs. Why don't you go up there and say something to him?" she suggests.

I walk upstairs and poke my head through the doorway of the 10-year-old's room. I don't immediately see him, but I know he's in there. I can hear breathing coming from underneath a mountain of *Mad* magazines, Sharper Image catalogs and overdue library books.

"I thought you were going to clean up your room," I say to the mountain.

"I hafta go to the bathroom first," a voice from beneath the mountain responds.

"Don't give me that. You just got out of the bathroom. Now, quit stalling and clean your room."

The 10-year-old, unfortunately, is not as easy to convince as the 13-year-old. Even though I have only been a member of this family for a few months, I have discovered that there is a major difference between them. The 13-year-old will listen to what I tell him to do, nod his head in agreement and then not do it. The 10-year-old will listen to what I tell him to do and argue for three hours before he doesn't do it. To the 13-year-old, arguing is just something to pass the time during MTV commercials. To the 10-year-old, it's a holy calling.

"Why do you care if it's not clean?" he argues. "It's *my* bedroom."

"I know it's your bedroom. The only reason I care is because I'm afraid the weight of all the junk you have in here is going to drop *your* bedroom into *our* living room."

"It's not junk. All of this is stuff I need."

"No one needs a roomful of damp bath towels, broken toys and candy bar wrappers. If you'd just throw away some of the things you don't use anymore, your room would be a lot neater. Why don't you start by getting rid of this guinea pig cage?"

"Why should I throw away Cotton's cage?"

"Because Cotton has been dead for two months."

"Are you sure?"

"Positive. The coroner listed the toxic fumes coming from under your bed as the probable cause of death."

"I suppose you've never heard of reincarnation?" he demands.

We spend the next three hours debating about which items can be thrown away and which ones he absolutely, positively cannot live without. Eventually we reach a compromise. The old magazines, broken toys and empty guinea pig cage will stay. But he's going to get rid of his clothes hamper and his waste basket.

It makes sense to me. They're the only things in his room we both know he's never going to use.

So far I am barely keeping my head above water in the sea of stepfatherhood, but I resolve to keep paddling.

A few days later my wife and I are in the kitchen, doing the dinner dishes. She is washing. I am drying. Her sons are in the living room, sprawled on the floor watching a *Cheers* rerun.

Finally, I can stand it no more.

"It's time for another change around here," I declare. "We should be the ones watching television and those two carpet potatoes should be out here doing the dishes."

"I'd rather do it myself," she says. "It's less hassle that way."

"There won't be any hassle," I assure her. "We just have to be firm."

The next night at the dinner table I introduce the subject of dishwashing to my stepsons.

"When I was your age," I begin, "I had certain chores to . . . "

"Is this the one about how you had to get up when it was still dark so you could feed the cows and milk the chickens before you went to school in the morning?" demands the 10-year-old.

"No, as a matter of fact, it isn't. This is the one about how I cleared the table every night, washed the dishes, put them away, cleaned the . . . "

"Is there a point to this nostalgia?" interrupts the 13-year-old. "I don't want to miss the beginning of *Cheers.*"

"The point is, from now on you guys are doing the dishes every night."

For the first time since I have sat at the head of this table, dinner is completed in silence. I have, I suspect, blown my shot at Stepfather of the Year. But I am determined to be firm. After dinner, their mother and I head for the living room to watch *Cheers*.

As Sam is attempting to inform us that "*Cheers* is filmed before a live studio audience," his words are drowned out by the sound of shouting from the kitchen. I get off the couch to investigate. My stepsons, the dishwashers, are standing on opposite sides of the table. In the middle of the table there is a spatula.

"He won't do his share," the 10-year-old yells.

"I do the dishes and you do the silverware," the 13-year-old yells back.

"That's not silverware. It's plastic."

"It's not a dish, either."

Before they will reach agreement on this one, I realize, that spatula will sprout legs, walk to the sink and wash itself.

"All right, you guys, it's obvious that this arrangement isn't going to work. Starting tomorrow, you can take turns doing the dishes."

The following night is the 13-year-old's turn. We go to the living room to watch television, leaving him in front of the sink. Before the *Cheers* crowd has a chance to shout "Norm," there is a 13-year-old sitting on the couch next to us.

"You're supposed to be doing the dishes," I point out.

"I'm done," he says.

I go to the kitchen to check it out. The dinner table is clear, but on top of the stove are two skillets and a roasting pan big enough to cook a water buffalo.

"What about these pans?" I ask him.

"I didn't see them," he swears.

I return to the living room. Before Carla has a chance to call Diane a bleachbag, the 13-year-old is back in the living room.

"The pans are clean," he says.

I walk back to the kitchen. Fortunately, I am wearing rubber-soled shoes, which probably is all that prevents me from slipping in the water on the kitchen floor and sliding out the back door.

I summon the 13-year-old.

"What about the water on the floor?" I demand.

"It's just a few drops," he contends.

"The cat is doing the backstroke past the refrigerator."

"You want me to clean it up?"

"No. I thought we'd bring in some coolies and have them plant rice."

The following night it is the 10-year-old's turn to do the dishes. As we leave the kitchen, he is standing in front of the sink. When we arrive in the living room, he is sitting on the couch.

"What about the dishes?" I say.

"They're done."

"They can't be done."

"They're done," he insists. "Why don't you ever believe me?"

"Because you're 10," I explain.

I march him to the kitchen. The first thing I notice is that the dishwasher is running. The second thing I notice is that it can't be real full, because on the table there are four glasses, four sets of silverware and a variety of serving bowls, all dirty.

"What about this stuff?" I demand.

"You said to do the dishes" he replies. "Glasses, bowls and silverware aren't dishes." If I'm ever on trial for insider trading, I want the 10-year-old as my attorney.

"Maybe not, but they are dirty. And as long as the dishwasher is running anyway, why don't you just slip them in there?" I suggest. "There's no sense wasting all that soap and water."

"Soap?" he says.

As a stepfather, I may be in over my head.

# STEPMOMS

No group of females ever has suffered lousier public relations than stepmothers.

Mothers are sacred. Grandmothers are kindly. Little girls are made of sugar and spice. Even prostitutes have hearts of gold.

But if the word that comes most often before mother is "sainted," the word that comes most often before stepmother is "wicked."

It's bad enough that we tell jokes about our mothers-in-law. But we tell horror stories about our stepmothers. It was a stepmother who forced Cinderella to stay home with her head up a chimney while her grody stepsisters went to the ball. It was a stepmother who sent Hansel and Gretel into the forest with a pocketful of bread crumbs.

We are fierce in our defense of motherhood. A mother can squander the grocery money on vodka, have Geraldo Rivera's phone number tattooed on her hip and spend her nights on the back of a Harley-Davidson. But say one bad word about her in front of her kids and you'll wake up two days later with knuckle marks all over your body. In some segments of our society, there is no greater slur than, "Yo' mama."

Ask any Irish tenor and he'll tell you that the quickest way to fill a room with sniffles is to break into, "M is for the many things she gave me . . ."

No one sings sentimental songs about stepmothers. Too often, a stepmother is "the other woman." An intruder in the family portrait. A snapshot in the back pages of the family photo album.

Stepmotherhood is not for the fainthearted. No woman marries a man because of his kids. She marries him in spite of them. The risks are too great and the rewards often are too small to be seen. No matter when or how or why you arrive on the scene, there is a good chance you will be regarded as a carpetbagger, capitalizing on a family's misfortune. If not the cause of it.

Your meals can be straight out of *Bon Appetit*, but they will not be as good as Mom's. No matter what rules you try to establish, they will not be the right ones. They will not be the way Mom does it.

And if, somehow, you survive the introduction to your stepkids, you never can be sure how long the honeymoon will last. You spend every day wondering if this is the one when you will hear, "You can't tell me what to do. You're not my real mother."

Not that motherhood is the bargain of the year. No matter how hard you work at it, you still might wind up with nothing more than a stranger who calls you biannually. But at least you had the early rewards, the memories that help absorb the shocks on the rough road ahead.

If you're a stepmother, you already have missed out on many of the moments that make it all worthwhile. Or, at least, survivable.

You didn't give them life. You never felt the first stirrings of their lives inside you. You never held them on your breast in the delivery room. You never nursed them, burped them or gazed down in awe at tiny fingers and incredibly delicate eyelashes.

Stepchildren come to you fully formed in someone else's image, with attitudes you did nothing to shape, achievements for which you cannot take credit, flaws that you had no chance to prevent. If you are lucky, they will come to you warily, hesitantly. If you are not so lucky, you will get them when they are hurting and confused and resentful.

It's a lousy deal in a lot of ways.

A stepmother knows that no matter how hard she tries, no matter how much she loves, she never will take the place of a real mother in a child's heart. She is the other woman. She always will be.

Any woman who accepts a deal like that deserves a few kind words, too.

# CHAPTER 5

○○○○○

In some ways, adjusting to stepfatherhood is easier for me than adjusting to stepmotherhood is for my wife.

I'd already had a lifetime of kids who were convinced that being told to clean off the dinner table was a violation of their civil rights and pushing a vacuum cleaner broke labor laws forbidding children to operate heavy machinery. I was used to kids who could out-argue Melvin Belli with one lip tied behind their back.

She, on the other hand, had no chance to prepare for the chaos my sons would bring to her condo when they were in my custody on weekends. Nor did she have a chance to brace herself for the influence my sons would have on her sons. Our kids may have been approximately the same ages, but there was one important difference: Her kids were Montessori graduates . . . my kids were Motley Crue dropouts.

Before we met, her sons dressed in Polo shirts, designer jeans and Dock Siders.

My sons lived in shredded T-shirts, baggy sweatpants and high-top tennis shoes.

Her sons spent Sunday afternoons taking walks in the woods with their mother, enjoying the quiet glories of nature.

My sons spent Sunday afternoons playing football in the mud with their father, until one of us lost a tooth.

Her sons read *Newsweek*, watched PBS and memorized the contents of the latest Sharper Image catalog.

My sons read the backs of Wheaties boxes, watched *Monday Night Football* and knew the point spreads on every game in the NFL.

Her sons engaged in lively discussions about current events at the dinner table.

My sons belched a lot.

"Don't worry," I assure her shortly after one of my sons has delivered an eruption that registers on the Richter scale. "Things will change. I'm sure that spending time with your boys will take some of the rough edges off mine."

"I hope so," she says. "I mean, your boys are very nice, but they are a bit rowdy."

"Yeah, I'm not sure why that is," I say, crushing my beer can on my forehead and lobbing it the length of the living room for a perfect three-pointer into her Waterford crystal bowl. "They probably got it from their mother."

Our conversation is interrupted by the sound of another enormous burp from the kitchen.

"That's disgusting," my wife says. "I wish you'd say something to him about it."

"Hey," I shout to the 15-year-old, "quit doing that. Your stepmother thinks it's disgusting."

"Hey," he shouts back, "it wasn't me."

"Who was it, then?"

Her 10-year-old appears in the doorway, a triumphant grin on his face.

"Me," he announces. "He taught me how. Cool, huh?"

I look at the 10-year-old's mother just in time to see her eyes rolling back in her head.

The blending process has begun. In no time at all, her sons are spending their Sunday afternoons playing football in the mud. They are reading Wheaties boxes and watching *Monday Night Football.* They are memorizing the point spread on all the NFL games. They can belch at will.

Of course, there are changes in my sons, too.

They still spend their Sundays playing football in the mud, of course. Only now they do it in Polo shirts, designer jeans and Dock Siders.

Football, in fact, probably is the perfect symbol for the differences in our families.

In my family, football always has been a way of life. All of my sons have played on organized teams. Most of our autumn weekends were spent in the backyard running post patterns and zig-outs. During the winter, there was not a lamp in our house that hadn't felt the sting of a Nerf football.

At her house, on the other hand, football was just another F word. She encouraged her sons to spend their time reading, writing and in other useless pursuits.

The inevitable culture collision takes place the first Sunday after the honeymoon.

"It's a great day outside," I note as the breakfast table is being cleared. "Let's get out there and find the nearest field."

"The boys will love that," she agrees. "But, instead of a field, why don't we go to the nature preserve? It has some beautiful wildflowers and the trees will be lovely at this time of year."

"Trees? Are you kidding? The ball will hit the branches."

"What ball?"

"The football. What did you think I meant?"

"I thought you wanted to take the boys outside to enjoy nature."

"Right. We're all going out to enjoy plenty of fresh air, sunshine and long bombs."

"I don't want my sons playing football," she declares. "It's dangerous."

"It's not dangerous."

"Then how come every time I see a game on television, they're always carrying some poor player off the field on a stretcher?"

"Insurance scams," I explain. "Besides, we're going to be playing touch football. Nobody gets hurt playing touch football."

"I still don't like it," she says. "I think the 10-year-old is too small to play football."

"Mothers always think their sons are too small to play football. William 'The Refrigerator' Perry's mother probably thinks he's too small to play football."

Reluctantly, she agrees to let her sons risk their lives and I take them to the nearest field for a game of two-hand touch. In three hours there are nine touchdowns, 17 interceptions and no injuries.

The following Sunday we go out for another football game. In three hours there are 12 touchdowns, 28 arguments and her 13-year-old gets a tiny cut over his left eye when he bumps heads with my 15-year-old.

"I knew it," she exclaims when we return home and she sees the cut. "He'll be scarred for the rest of his life. Hurry and get him into the car before he loses too much blood. I think I know a plastic surgeon who . . . "

"Take it easy," I say. "It's only a scratch. I've seen paper cuts that bled more than that."

The 13-year-old survives his wound and the next Sunday we go out for another game. The score is tied, 84-84, when I throw a pass to the 10-year-old. He catches it and streaks toward the end zone. Just as he reaches the goal line, he is caught from behind by my 12-year-old, flips into the air and comes down on his shoulder.

I take him to the emergency room, where X-rays reveal a small fracture in his collarbone. He will have to wear a sling for three weeks. It will be six weeks until the bone is entirely healed.

But that's not the worst part. The worst part is coming home and explaining to his mother that her 10-year-old's injury is not an insurance scam. The way I look at it, the kid is the lucky one.

The only thing *he* got in a sling was his arm.

Anyway, she'll just have to understand that football always has been a part of my fatherhood. As soon as they were old enough to get their backfields in motion, I began playing football with my kids.

In the beginning, we played on the living room floor. The sides were me against them and I had to play on my hands and knees. The games were close, but they always won, no matter how many times I had to fumble just before I would have scored the winning touchdown.

After a few years and a lot of broken lamps, our games moved to the backyard. The sides still were me against them and I was only allowed to run at half speed. The games stayed close, but they always won, no matter how many times I had to miss a tackle to make sure they could score the winning touchdown.

Eventually they grew. The sides became me and the littlest kid against the rest and I was only allowed to run at three-quarter speed. The games continued to be close, but they always won, no matter how many passes I had to throw directly into their hands to make sure they could catch one for the winning interception.

Once they became teen-agers, our football games grew less frequent and, for a while, they stopped altogether. But when my wife and I merge our leagues, football fever strikes my family once again. When enough time has elapsed for the 10-year-old's collarbone to heal — and for his mother to forget about it — the Sunday afternoon games resume.

By this time, however, another year has elapsed. They are another year older. And so, unfortunately, am I. On a warm fall afternoon when we are throwing the ball around a vacant lot to loosen up for the first game of the new season, I begin to realize that, for me, the future was yesterday.

When it is time to choose sides, the 16-year-old wins the coin toss and picks his 13-year-old brother . My 21-year-old, who has stopped by for the day, picks his 14-year-old stepbrother. The 16-year-old picks his 11-year-old stepbrother. The 21-year-old looks around. The only ones left in the vacant lot are me and a squirrel who is rooting around the field in search of last-minute nuts. There is a long pause while the 21-year-old thinks it over.

"It's my football," I remind him.

"Don't worry, I was going to pick you, anyway," he says. "It would take too long to teach the squirrel how to play zone defense."

The game begins with our team on defense.

"I'll cover the 16-year-old," I announce.

The 21-year-old snickers. The 14-year-old grins. The 16-year-old falls on the ground and rolls around, clutching his stomach and laughing hysterically. When the ball is snapped, the 16-year-old still is rolling on the ground. The next thing I know, the 16-year-old is rolling on the ground in the end zone, clutching the ball with one hand and his stomach with the other. He still is laughing hysterically. Not only can he run faster than I can run, he can *roll* faster than I can run.

Then it's our turn to go on offense. The 21-year-old calls the play.

"You run down about 30 yards and if you're open I'll hit you," he instructs me.

"How about if I run the first 15 yards and then walk the rest of the way?" I wheeze.

"I knew I should have picked the squirrel," he says.

I trot up to the line of scrimmage. As a sign of their respect, the opposing team has assigned the 11-year-old to cover me. Our center hikes the ball. I start to run. Not only do I not get open, I do not get 30 yards down the field. Somewhere around the 12-yard mark, a muscle in the back of my leg decides that a man my age does not belong on a football field with a bunch of kids who can make it from one end zone to the other without stopping for a nap. The muscle ties itelf into a knot and I hit the ground like a bad pass.

I crawl to the sidelines and watch the rest of the game from there. If those kids ever expect to get me back out on the field, they're just going to have to learn to get down on their hands and knees and fumble the ball to make sure I score the winning touchdown.

Stepfatherhood, I am forced to admit that day, may be a little different than fatherhood was, after all.

When I kicked off, fatherhood was 18 years of Olympic Games and there were guys competing in decathlons who didn't get as much exercise as I did. I can't remember a weekend with my first son that didn't involve throwing, catching, running and liniment.

Looking back, I realize the only reason I survived was because I was in my 30s. When my knees bent, they did not pop like cheap firecrackers. If I threw a football on Sunday, I did not come to the office with my arm in a sling on Monday.

Now that I am in the end zone of fatherhood, times, and my body, have changed a bit. I may have reached a point where I will have to limit my weekend athletic plans to baseball, basketball and bowling. Even then, I may have to pace myself to be able to watch all three of them without falling asleep on the couch.

Which is what I am trying to do one weekend when my 13-year-old walks into the living room dribbling a basketball.

"Hep, Pops," he says, "how about shooting some hoops?"

"I was going to watch television," I inform him.

"Don't you want to get some exercise?"

"I *am* going to get some exercise. During the seventh inning stretch, I'm probably going to have to get off the couch and let the cat out."

"OK," he says, "never mind. I'll find somone else to shoot baskets with. There probably are some guys down at the playground who can give me a *real* game of one-on-one."

"What's that supposed to mean?" I demand.

"Oh, nothing," he says. "I mean, you do all right for a guy of your age. But it's not really much of a challenge beating you anymore."

"We'll see about that," I say. I get off the couch and trot outside. We walk to the playground and play a 100-point game. Of which six points are mine.

I return home. Perspiration still is rolling down my face when the 11-year-old walks into the living room.

"Will you help me fly my kite?" he asks. "It's too big for me to get into the air by myself."

I get off the couch and trudge outside. Not only is the 11-year-old's kite too big for him to handle by himself, it is too big to land at O'Hare.

"You run with it and I'll hold the end of the string," the 11-year-old says.

I pick up the kite and begin to run with it. By the time the kite is in the air, I have run far enough to qualify for the Boston Marathon. I leave the 11-year-old hanging onto his string and return to the condo.

Oxygen still is making its way back to my lungs when the 14-year-old walks into the living room.

"Wanna hit some tennis balls?" he asks.

I get off the couch and crawl outside. For an hour I hit tennis balls to the 14-year-old and chase after the ones he hits back. Twenty-five percent of the ones he hits back do not land in our court. Thirty-five percent of the ones he hits back do not land in our county. The only chance we have of seeing some of those balls again is if their pictures appear on milk cartons.

When the last ball has been lost, I return home and collapse on the couch. I can't wait for the next kid to walk into the living room. I'm going to need his help to operate the channel changer.

My wife could be right, I am forced to admit. There's a lot to be said for quiet walks in the woods, sniffing wildflowers and looking at trees.

But even if my kids weren't into violent sports, my wife still would have to learn to adjust to the violence they bring to the dinner table. Not that there is a great deal of difference. In many ways, in fact, it's safer on the football field. At least nobody in the huddle is packing salad forks.

I'm not sure how the dining room wound up being the most dangerous room in our house. As nearly as I can recall, the mealtimes of my childhood were quiet, dignified events. My father wore a suit and tie, my mother wore pearls and high heels and I washed my hands and face for at least an hour before I came to the table. I spoke only when spoken to, smiled when my mother passed a second helping of asparagus-liver casserole and wouldn't leave the table until I was excused, even if my chair had burst into flames.

Or maybe that was Beaver Cleaver's childhood.

Either way, the mealtimes of my childhood were nothing like the mealtimes of my parenthood. Especially when there are four sets of unwashed elbows on the table at the same time.

The first time our combined family sits down together is a few weeks after the wedding. The meal gets off to a slow start when I announce that dinner will be on the table in 10 minutes. Half an hour later, four kids who have been "starving to death" since five minutes past lunch begin to show up. Two of them are not wearing shirts. One of them is not wearing pants.

When they all are clothed and seated, my wife carries a bowl of mashed potatoes and a platter of fried chicken into the dining room. Before the dishes touch the tablecloth, three hands — two of which have not been washed since the Carter administration — grab for drumsticks.

My 15-year-old, who is the strongest, gets one. Her 10-year-old, who is the smallest but the sneakiest, gets the other. My 12-year-old winds up with a neck. He immediately punches her 10-year-old on the shoulder, knocking him sideways out of his chair. While he lies on the floor, clutching his shoulder and screaming for a medic, her 13-year-old grabs the 10-year-old's drumstick and eats it. Bone and all.

My wife glares at me.

"Aren't you going to say something?" she demands. "We haven't even said grace and already they're beating each other up."

"Don't beat up your stepbrother before we say grace," I tell the 12-year-old.

We say grace. While our heads are bowed, someone makes a crude sound. This apparently qualifies as state-of-the-art humor to my 15-year-old, who topples sideways out of his chair, laughing. While he is rolling on the floor, her 13-year-old grabs his drumstick and eats it.

Finally grace is survived and everyone is seated again. There are two seconds of silence before my 12-year-old groans, "Oh, sick."

"What's sick?" I ask, not really wanting to know.

"This salad has onions in it." The 12-year-old has a thing about onions. He's the only person I know who brings a jeweler's loupe to the table to examine his food for microscopic onion pieces.

"Why don't you take them out and eat just the lettuce?" my wife asks.

"I'm not touching those things," he says.

"You don't have to touch them," I point out. "Just fall out of your chair and the 13-year-old will steal them off your plate."

The debate about whether there is life after onions is interrupted by her 10-year-old's shout of, "Oh, gross. Make him stop."

"What's the problem?" I ask.

"He mixed his green beans into his apple sauce," the 10-year-old moans. "That's disgustable. I'm gonna gag my brains out."

"He's a very sensitive child," his mother explains.

"Yeah," the sensitive child says. "I had two pieces of bread, 28 green beans and four spoons of mashed potatoes in my mouth when I saw what he was doing and I started choking and I was afraid the potatoes were gonna shoot out my nose and the green beans were . . . "

"We get the picture," I interrupt, not sure how much more sensitivity I can stand before I gag *my* brains out. At times like these, I have to keep reminding myself that Beaver Cleaver's childhood was a creation of someone's imagination.

And so, I suspect, was mine.

But then, squaring the black-and-white world of the old family sitcoms with the black-and-blue reality of actual family life always has been a major problem for me. I need to remember that there never really was a time when father knew best. Any program that included a "family meeting scene," for instance, was never meant to be taken seriously.

Family meeting scenes have been a staple of sitcoms ever since the first time Jim and Margaret Anderson sat down with their kids to discuss whether it was all right for Bud to eat more than one chocolate chip cookie before dinner.

The topics varied, but the form always was the same. Dad stood in front of the fireplace with his elbow resting on the mantel. Mom sat on a chair with a cup of tea in her lap. The kids sat at attention on the sofa. Wearing their Confirmation clothes.

"Gee, Dad, what do you want to talk to us about?" the kids would ask.

Dad would talk. The kids would listen. Mom would nod her head in agreement. At the end of the meeting, the kids would say, in unison, "Gee, Dad, I guess you're right."

If you don't think a scene like that is hysterical, you're a bachelor and your parents' names probably were Ozzie and Harriet. Because, in the real world, family meetings are like the first one we have shortly after our two little families combine to become one large feud.

The topic is: which restaurant should we go to for dinner? Personally, I am not in favor of taking kids to restaurants until they are old enough to pick up the check. But my wife suggests that going out to dinner would be a perfect way for all of us to get to know each other a little better.

"Where do you want to go?" I ask.

"I don't know," she replies. "Why don't we let the kids decide? We can have a family meeting. It will be just like the Brady Bunch."

I yell for the kids to come into the living room. My 15-year-old arrives first. He is not wearing his Confirmation clothes. He is wearing a pair of Jams that reach his knees and a T-shirt with an obscene message written in Spanish across the chest. He sprawls on the couch.

Her 13-year-old comes in next. He is wearing his underwear. And my socks. He sprawls on the other end of the couch.

My 12-year-old follows them. He is wearing three-day-old sweat pants with the knees torn out. He sprawls in the middle of the couch.

Her 10-year-old wanders in last. He is wearing Jams that reach his ankles and three-day-old dirt. There is no room left for him on the couch. He sprawls on top of the other kids.

I stand in front of the television, which, I am pretty sure, is the only way I will get them to look in my direction. Mom sits in a chair with a glass of wine in her lap. We do not look like the Brady Bunch, exactly. But we do bear a strong resemblance to the Manson family.

"Okay, old dude, we're all here," one of the kids says. "Whaddya want this time?"

"We're going out for dinner tonight," I explain. "Let's decide where."

"How about Chinese food?" my 15-year-old suggests.

"Chinese food reeks," says my 12-year-old. The 15-year-old punches him on the arm. The 12-year-old swings back and accidentally hits her 13-year-old. Her 13-year-old kicks her 10-year-old on purpose.

Mom takes a sip of her wine.

"All right, knock it off you guys and let's hear another suggestion," I say.

"Mexican food,"says her 13-year-old.

"Mexican food is slime," says my 15-year-old. Her 13-year-old punches him on the leg. My 15-year-old winds up and crocks my 12-year-old. All three of them kick her 10-year-old. Being the littlest brother is a high-risk profession.

Mom drains her glass of wine.

"If you guys don't stop fighting, we're just going to stay home and have pizza delivered," I warn them.

"Pepperoni," shouts my 12-year-old. My 15-year-old punches him in the stomach. Her 13-year-old punches him in the back. Her 10-year-old jumps off the couch and punches the cat.

Mom is chugging her wine straight from the bottle.

I stand with my elbow on the television and survey the scene. The 15-year-old has bruised knuckles. The 13-year-old is bleeding. The 12-year-old is gasping for air. The 10-year-old is crying. The cat is hissing. Mom is sliding out of her chair clutching an empty wine bottle.

If we ever have another family meeting, I decide, we're not inviting any kids.

My wife and I could — and probably will — debate forever about how real boys are supposed to act. But every once in a while, even she has to concede that I have the benefit of experience. When she is planning her youngest kid's birthday party, for instance, I know right away she is on the wrong track when she asks me about the napkins.

"Which do you like better?" she asks. "The mauve napkins with the butterfly motif or the taupe ones edged with wildflowers?"

"Well, it depends," I hedge, not willing to commit myself to such a significant decision without knowing all the details. "What are the napkins for?"

"My 11-year-old's birthday party," she says.

"C'mon, quit kidding," I chortle. "You don't really expect me to believe you're buying napkins for an 11-year-old boy's birthday party."

"Why would I be kidding? When you serve cake, ice cream and soft drinks to people, you need napkins."

"Sure, when you serve them to *people,*" I agree. "But when you serve cake, ice cream and soft drinks to 11-year-old boys, you don't need napkins. You need a fire hose."

"Now you're the one who's kidding."

"You think so? When my third kid had his 11th birthday party, one of the guests got so covered with cake frosting we had to chip air holes in it so he could breathe until the rescue squad got there with the Jaws of Life. And another kid lost three fingers to frostbite from spending the entire party with his hand buried in the ice cream carton. And we still get calls once a week from the parents of the two missing children who . . . "

"This party isn't going to be anything like that," she interrupts. "All of his friends come from fine families and are very well-behaved."

"I don't care if they're all direct descendents of Emily Post and came over on the Mayflower. You get a roomful of 11-year-old boys together and there isn't a homeowner's insurance policy in the world that will cover you."

"Without proper supervision I suppose they can get a little rambunctious," she concedes. "The secret is to make sure things stay under control."

"Does that mean you've hired a SWAT team?"

"It means I've planned enough activities to keep them busy. The first thing we'll do when they arrive is have the 11-year-old open presents."

"Good. That'll kill 10 or 15 seconds."

"After that we'll have the cake and ice cream and then they can watch a movie on the VCR. I've already called the video rental store and reserved *Sound of Music.* When the movie's over we'll . . . "

"Hold it," I butt in. "You've called the video rental store and reserved what?"

"*Sound of Music.* They'll love it. I know I loved it when I was 11."

"Of course you did. You were a girl and that was a long, uh, a few years ago. Times are different and so are boys. The only way they're going to love *Sound of Music* is if you can find a version where the entire von Trapp family gets locked in a house on Elm Street and they get chain sawed into bite-sized pieces by a guy wearing a hockey mask."

Despite my advice, she goes ahead with her original plans for the birthday party. When the kids arrive, she seats them all in the dining room and we watch while the 11-year-old breaks the 10-second barrier ripping open his packages. His favorite present is a box that contains enough fireworks to blow up Riverfront Stadium.

"Cool," he shouts, grabbing a handful of bottle rockets and leading a stampede to the backyard. While *Sound of Music* sits unplayed on the VCR, the patio is alive with the sound of fireworks. By the time the party is over, the well-behaved children from fine families have proved that it is not possible to shoot down a moving starling with a nine-inch bottle rocket. But it is possible for a 12-inch mini-missile to be launched from the center of a three-layer birthday cake without melting the little icing flowers around the edges.

She was right about one thing, though. The mauve napkins with the butterflies were a big hit. One kid ate nine of them.

Despite our differing views of children, we do reach agreement on one issue when her son turns 11, proving that parental theories may vary from family to family, but some rules are written in stone.

When a kid does not finish his dinner, a parent is required by federal law to point out that there are children starving in India.

When a kid complains it is too far to walk to school, it is illegal for a parent not to begin his or her reply with, "When I was your age . . . "

And when a kid asks for a BB gun for his birthday, a parent faces a term of not less than 10 years in prison and a fine of not more than $5,000 if he or she does not immediately declare, "Absolutely not. You'll shoot your eye out."

So when the 11-year-old hands us a gift list for his birthday that begins and ends with "BB gun," his mother and I simultaneously, and without rehearsal, break into a chorus of the Missing Eyeball Overture.

It probably would have been easier to do the 10 years in jail.

"I won't shoot my eye out," he insists.

"Yes you will," I reply. "Kids who get BB guns always shoot their eyes out."

"Name one."

"What?"

"Name one kid who ever shot his eye out with a BB gun," he challenges.

His mother and I stare at each other, unable to come up with an answer. Just because we have been parents for a long time doesn't mean we are good at it. We adjourn to the kitchen to talk it over.

"Quick," she says, "think of somebody who shot his eye out with a BB gun when you were a kid."

"I can't think of anybody. How about you?"

"Girls never wanted BB guns when I was a kid," she points out. "I do remember Judy Rich getting a nasty eye injury when we were in fifth grade. But I think she got that from poking herself with an eyebrow pencil."

"How about Moshe Dyan?" I ask her. "I think I read somewhere that his parents gave him a BB gun."

"I don't think so, but you may be on the right track," she replies. "Think of somebody else who wears an eye patch."

"Well, there's the guy in the Hathaway shirt ads."

"Get serious," she says. "If we don't come up with a good answer, we're going to wind up with a front yard full of wounded tin cans."

"How about if we're just honest with him about it and admit that we can't think of anyone who ever shot out his eye, but that doesn't mean it couldn't happen?"

"It's worth a try," she agrees. "I've always felt honesty is the best policy."

"Honesty," I agree.

We walk back into the living room.

"We can think of dozens of kids who shot out their eyes with BB guns," I tell the 11-year-old. "But, even if we couldn't, we wouldn't want to take a chance of it happening to you."

"It's impossible," he says.

"What's impossible?"

"It's impossible for me to shoot out my eye with a BB gun. Look at it logically. The gun is about three feet long. My arms are only two feet long. Even if I wanted to shoot out my eye, I wouldn't be able to point the gun at myself and reach the trigger."

His mother and I stare at each other a moment and then return to the kitchen.

"Now what?" I ask.

"I saw an ad for BB guns at the Toy Emporium."

"I'll pick one up on my way home from work tomorrow."

Even when we do agree on how kids should be handled, it really doesn't matter a great deal. Not to the kids, anyway.

PREFACE: CHAPTER 6

# SHOPPING FOR COMMON INTERESTS

One problem with getting remarried is that you have to go through the whole process of education all over again.

After 22 years, I was just beginning to make noticeable progress in my first marriage. She had learned that Super Bowl Sunday was not a good time to have a Tupperware party in our living room. She no longer burst into tears when the seven-course dinner she had spent all day preparing wound up being inhaled during the two-minute warning. She stopped expecting me to talk during the World Series, the Masters, Wimbledon, the Stanley Cup playoffs, the NCAA Final Four basketball tournament or the finals of the World Tractor Pulling championships.

Now I have to go through the entire routine again.

I'd forgotten how big the job can be until the day my first draft choice walks into the living room while I am watching a rerun of the 1986 Full Contact Karate Tournament.

"Guess what?" she asks.

"What, my darling?" I reply, taking my eyes away from the screen to glance briefly at her. Which should assure her that there still is fire in our romance.

"We've been invited to a pool party."

"Wonderful, sweetheart," I say, trying not to be distracted by the fact that the guy in white pants has just delivered a terrific kick to his opponent's left ear. "When is it?"

"Sunday."

"This Sunday, my angel?"

"Yes."

"Are you crazy . . . dear?" I scream. "You actually accepted an invitation to a party on the day my favorite basketball team is fighting for its life in the NBA playoffs?"

"You mean basketball season is still going?"

"Why wouldn't it be? It's only June."

"But I could have sworn it ended last week. I distinctly remember you jumping off the couch and screaming, 'We win the series!' when the game was over. In fact, there's still a beer stain on the carpet."

"That was the Eastern Conference series," I explain, trying to be patient with her. When it comes to sports, not all women are possessed of the type of logic needed to deal with the way these things work. I still can remember how difficult it was for my first wife to understand that, even though the Cincinnati Reds were champions of the West Division, they wouldn't necessarily qualify for the World Series unless they defeated the St. Louis Cardinals, who were the champions of the East Division. Every time I'd try to explain it, I'd get frustrated and she'd mutter something about "geography dropouts" before walking out of the room.

This time, however, I am determined to remain calm and even-tempered. This woman is, after all, the most important thing that has come into my life since the three-point field goal.

I put my arms around her, gently move her so that she is not standing directly in front of the screen, and quietly outline the facts of professional basketball life.

"Well, I certainly hope all this basketball stuff gets done before the wedding," she says when I have finished. "I'd hate to have you miss an important game just because of something as trivial as our honeymoon."

"Uh, now that you mention it, that brings up something I've been meaning to speak with you about," I admit. "I just checked the schedule and I noticed that the first game of the Cleveland Browns' exhibition season is the day after our wedding."

"What are you telling me?" she demands. "That you want to delay the honeymoon because of some stupid baseball game?"

The woman has a lot to learn. But then, so do I.

# CHAPTER 6

# OOOOOO

One of the keys to a successful marriage, we agreed, was to at least make an attempt to share each other's interests. Sharing each other's interests, we knew from experience, would lead to improved communication, mutual respect and a lifetime of marital bliss.

I have done my best to live up to my part of the bargain.

I have gone with her to art museums to stare at paintings that may or may not be hanging right side up. I have accompanied her to trendy boutiques and attempted not to snicker while she tried on the latest creations by Italian sissies. I have clutched my chest in trendy boutiques and waited for my heartbeat to resume after seeing the price tags on the latest creations by Italian sissies.

After a year or so of marital bliss, I mention that it might be time for her to try sharing one of my interests.

"After all," I point out, "there's more to life than culture, refinement and good taste."

"Like what?" she asks.

"Football."

"I don't think I ever could get interested in football," she says. "I don't understand a thing about it."

"That never stopped Howard Cosell. Anyway, it's really a very simple game."

"If it's such a simple game, how come every time that fat guy with the loud voice diagrams a play on television, the screen winds up looking like a second-grader scribbled on it?"

"Fat guy?"

"You know, John Madman."
"His name's not Madman. It's Madden."
"Well, he sounds like a madman. And he's a terrible dresser."
"OK, maybe his diagrams are a little confusing," I allow. "But nobody really cares what the pulling guard is doing to the strong side linebacker anyway. All you really need to know is a few basics."
I take a piece of paper and draw 22 X's and O's.
"Now," I explain, "these O's represent the defensive players."
"What do they do?"
"They try to find whoever has the ball and tackle him."
"Who do the X's tackle?"
"They don't tackle anybody. They're not allowed to. Their job is to try to keep whoever has the ball from being knocked down."
"They sound like caring and sensitive people."
"I'm sure they are," I agree. "See this X in the middle?"
"Yes."
"He's called the center."
"That makes sense, I guess," she says.
"I told you it was a simple game. Now, the X next to the center is called the guard. And next to the guard is the tackle. And next to the tackle you have the . . . "
"Why?"
"Why what?"
"Why is that X called the tackle? You said the X's aren't allowed to tackle anybody. If he can't tackle anybody, why is he called a tackle?"
"How should I know?" I exclaim. "Maybe they ran out of names. What a stupid question."
"You don't have to yell."
"I'm not yelling. I'm explaining."
"Well you don't have to explain so loudly. You're starting to sound like John Madman."
I pick up the piece of paper with the X's and O's on it and slowly crumple it into a little ball. The road to marital bliss, I suspect, does not necessarily have an exit ramp leading to a football field. Anyway, some interests probably are just too important to share with a spouse.
Her interest in football is roughly the same as my interest in fashion. Of course, I knew about this difference between us long before we got married. On the night we got engaged, in fact, she put her arms around me and held me tight. Her lips came close to my ear. Her voice was soft and low as she whispered:
"Sweetheart?"
"Yes, my love?"
"Where did you get those ugly socks?"
"What?"
"Those socks. Where did you get them? And why on earth would you

wear them in public?"

"What's wrong with my socks?"

"Oh, nothing, I guess. It's just that they're, well, tan. Tan socks don't go very well with blue slacks."

"I know that. But my green socks are in the wash."

She is silent for the rest of the evening. Which, I assume, indicates that she is satisfied I am in pretty firm control of my life, clothes-wise. But the next day she mentions the subject again.

"Don't get me wrong, you always look very nice," she begins, "but your wardrobe really could use just a tiny bit of help. After all, clothes should make a statement."

"My clothes *are* making a statement," I remind her. "They're stating that I have an ex-wife who gets alimony payments, two kids who get child support payments and another kid going to a college where the bursar puts in 12-hour days sending out tuition bills. Besides, it's not as if I don't already have enough clothes. I've got a whole closet full of them. Go look for yourself."

She goes into my bedroom to browse through my closet. A few minutes later she returns to the living room.

"Well?" I ask.

"I always wondered where old leisure suits went to die," she mutters.

"OK, so they're not all exactly up to the standards of Ralph Lauren," I admit.

"They're not exactly up to the standards of Ralph Kramden," she counters.

"Clothes aren't that important to me," I admit. "As far as I'm concerned, clothes are meant to help you stay warm and hide bulges. Besides, I really don't have time to fool around buying clothes. By the time I get to the shopping center and find a place to park and get inside and wait for the blue light to start flash . . . "

"Let me get a couple of things for you," she interrupts. "It'll be sort of an early wedding present."

A few days later she shows up at my apartment with an armload of packages for me. I open the top package. Inside there is a pair of socks. They are a shade of blue not found in Mother Nature's crayon box.

"Like them?" she asks.

"I've always wanted socks that glowed in the dark," I say.

"They'll go great with the rest of the things I picked out," she says, handing me another package. "Guess what this is."

"I can't guess," I admit. I open the package and look at the contents.

I still can't guess.

It has the shape of a sweater, but it is not any color that nature intended a sweater to be. It is a dozen different glaring colors, splashed around at random. It looks like a vandalized neon sign.

"It's a Coogi," she says.

"Thank heaven. For a minute there, I was afraid you were going to tell me it was a sweater."

"It *is* a sweater," she says. "Coogi is the brand name. They're the very latest thing from Australia. Don't you love it?"

"Love might be a little strong," I admit. "But maybe I'll respect it in the morning."

"If you don't like it, I can take it back. It was pretty expensive."

Immediately I realize that, no matter what this sweater looks like, we aren't talking bargain basement sales here. This is not a woman who uses the phrase "pretty expensive" lightly. I have heard her refer to the Hope diamond as ``up-scale."

And I don't want to hurt her feelings. It's just that it is not a sweater I would have picked out. I am a gray sweater kind of guy. Which is not to say my taste in clothes is mundane. In my lifetime I also have purchased several tan sweaters. Once, in a particularly memorable shopping binge, my impulsive nature took over and I bought a navy blue sweater.

But seeing as she went to all the trouble of buying it for me, I might as well wear it. So what if it looks like an MTV test pattern? I can handle a little bit of snickering.

The next day I wear the sweater to work. I walk into the office and hang up my coat. Before I can reach my desk, a co-worker looks up from her newspaper and says, "Great sweater."

I brace myself, waiting for the punch line. While I am waiting, another co-worker walks past.

"Nice sweater," he says.

I look closely at both of them. Neither one is snickering.

In the next half hour there is a parade of co-workers walking past my desk and making flattering remarks about my sweater. People who haven't talked to me in years stop me in the hall to tell me they love my sweater. Total strangers call me on the phone to tell me they have heard about my sweater. On the elevator, a businessman wearing an expensive-looking suit and a Rolex glances at me and enthuses, "Terrific Coogi. I'm saving up for one of my own."

As we head toward the wedding day, my wardrobe continues to change.

Shirts with little men on horseback begin to appear in my dresser drawers in place of T-shirts testifying that I have visited Disneyworld, Dollywood and the World Spam Eating Championship.

Perfectly comfortable Expand-O-Matic pants give way to slacks created by French designers of indeterminate gender. My Joe Namath all-weather reversible plaid sport coat gets pushed to the back of the closet to make room for a baggy silk suit designed by some guy named Georgio.

Even worse, clothes I have worn and loved through several Presidential administrations begin to disappear. My officially licensed Cleveland

Browns jersey with the picture of Brian Sipe on the back vanishes. My brown and green necktie, woven of 100 percent polyester, goes AWOL. When I ask her about these missing items, she smiles innocently and says, "I don't know, dear. Maybe the Good Taste Fairy came and took them away."

Not only is there a drastic change in the clothes I am supposed to wear, there are new rules for how I am supposed to wear them. The difference goes all the way down to my socks.

I'm not sure why this surprises me. My whole life has been an endless search for good socks.

When I was a kid, my socks lasted for about two weeks before the elastic wore out and they no longer would stay up. No matter how often I tugged on them, with each step they would slip a little farther down my ankles until eventually they disappeared entirely inside the heels of my shoes.

My mother said it was my fault.

"You put them on wrong," she would insist.

"How can I put them on wrong? Socks only go one way."

"Don't get smart with me, little boy."

As I got older, elastic manufacturers improved their product and my socks stayed up longer. Which only meant more time for holes to develop in them.

My mother blamed the holes on me.

"Do you know why there are holes in your socks?" she would demand, slipping one over her hand and letting a finger wiggle through the hole.

"Why?" I would ask.

"Because you don't trim your toenails, that's why."

"This sock has a hole in the back," I would point out. "What am I supposed to do about that, trim my heels?"

"Don't get smart with me, young man."

By the time of my first marriage, socks were made of sterner stuff and did not wear out at all. Which only meant there were more opportunities for one of each pair to disappear.

My wife-du-jour insisted that I was doing something wrong.

"If you'd put them both in the hamper at the same time, they wouldn't get lost," she would declare.

"Oh, right. Like the way I do it now is that I take off a sock and put it in the hamper and then walk around with the other one on for a few days before I get around to throwing it in, too."

"Don't get smart with me, buster."

Eventually I solved the orphan sock problem by buying only black socks. By the time of my divorce, I had cornered the black sock market. Which only meant that I was hopelessly out of fashion, because well-dressed men seldom wore black socks anymore.

My friends urged me to buy trendier socks. So I went to a store where they sold socks for the price of shoes and a salesman showed me the latest in foot coverings.

"This sock is very witty," he said, holding up a red and green argyle.

"I don't care if it's witty," I replied. "I seldom have conversations with my socks."

"There's no need to get smart with me, sir."

Now I have a drawer full of socks that are trendier than Cher and witty enough to guest host for Arsenio Hall. Which still doesn't mean that I have a satisfactory socks life. Because shortly before our wedding we are at a tennis party when my future socks partner pulls me aside and hisses:

"Fix your socks."

"Why?" I hiss back, "are they broken?"

"This is no time to get smart with me, sweetheart. People are staring at your socks. If they were pulled up any higher, they'd be around your waist."

"What's wrong with that?"

"*Nobody* wears their socks pulled up any more. You've got to push them down around your ankles."

I start to tell her about how my socks used to slide down around my ankles all by themselves when I was a kid and how I couldn't wait to be able to afford socks that would stay up. And that if I push my socks down, people won't know if it's because I'm trendy or because I'm too poor to own socks with elastic in them. But I realize I would be wasting my breath. As usual, my socks life is a mess and there probably is only one thing left for me to do.

Before the wedding, I'm going to have to see a socks therapist.

But the most dramatic change in my wardrobe doesn't come until after we are married and I am moving my clothes into our combined closet.

"Sweetheart?" she asks, as I am hanging my Perry Ellis single-breasted ventless sport coat next to my Alexander Julian button-down shirt with the teal striping.

"Yes, my love?"

"Where's your tuxedo?"

"Don't worry. I'm almost positive I returned it to the rental place after the wedding. At least, I certainly hope so. After all this time, the late charges would be pretty steep."

"Are you trying to tell me that you don't *own* a tuxedo?"

"Why would I want to *own* a tuxedo? I'm not planning to get married again any time soon. And I'm pretty sure I'm not going to get invited to any more proms."

"Tuxedos aren't just for weddings and proms. What about black tie social events?"

"What black tie social events?"

"The Art Ball, for instance. If you owned your own tuxedo, think of the money you'd save by not having to rent one every year for that."

"I've already saved a lot of money," I point out. "I've never gone to the Art Ball."

"Come on, don't kid about something like that."

"Who's kidding? I've never gone to the Art Ball. I think it's always on my bowling night."

"OK, then, how about the Performing Arts Fund Raiser?"

"I guess I'm not on their mailing list."

"The Friends of the Ballet Winter Gala?"

"Is that the one where the tickets begin at $500 and if you drive an American car they request that you car pool with someone who owns a Porsche?"

"That's the one."

"Nope, I don't go to that one, either. Looks like there's no sense in me owning a tux."

And that, I assume, is the end of the tuxedo topic. Which proves that I don't know any more about this marriage than I did about the last one.

Because two weeks later a delivery truck arrives with a package for me. Inside is a black tuxedo designed by some guy named Adolfo. It is, to be honest, a very nice tuxedo and could come in quite handy if Manpower ever has an opening for a temporary maitre d'.

My only problem now is getting it into my closet. I just hope she doesn't suggest that I throw out my Nehru jacket to make room for it.

Fortunately, it never comes to that. Because I have four kids standing in line at my closet door to keep my clothes population under control.

When I was single and bought all my own clothes , that never was a problem. My sons would have appeared in public wearing flowered dresses and open-toed high heels rather than put on anything of mine. But when word gets out that my wife has begun selecting my wardrobe, my closet turns into a lending library filled with empty hangers.

The remarkable thing is that one of my sons is three inches shorter than I am and built like a Bulgarian weight lifter, while another is three inches taller than I am and built like an Ethiopian basketball player. But when they're raiding my closet, one size fits all. As I discover as we are getting ready to go out one evening for an informal dinner.

"What are you going to wear?" my wife asks.

"I'm not sure," I admit, surveying my fraction of our walk-in closet. "It's a tossup between my new tuxedo and my old softball uniform. Do you think this restaurant has a policy against cleats?"

"What are you talking about? Why would you wear cleats to a restaurant when you have three pairs of Reeboks that would go perfectly with just about any outfit you want to wear?"

"And I have five sons, four of whom have not been able to find their own shoes since their feet became the same size as mine. Not that it would matter. Even if I had a pair of shoes, I wouldn't have anything to wear with them."

"That's impossible," she exclaims. "I've bought dozens of new things for you since we've been married. What about the tan cords I bought you for your birthday? They'd go perfectly with your new bulky sweater."

"The last time I saw my tan cords, they were walking out the door on the 16-year-old. He didn't even bother to cut off the tags. And the 21-year-old stopped by last week to borrow the bulky sweater."

"You let him take your brand new sweater?"

"I had to. He didn't have anything to wear over my brand new Polo shirt."

"Well, then, I suppose you could go a little more casual. You could wear your Hard Rock Cafe sweatshirt with a pair of stone-washed jeans."

"No good. The 14-year-old is wearing my Hard Rock Cafe sweatshirt to a football game. And my stone-washed jeans are spending tonight hanging out in McDonald's parking lot. The next time I see them, they'll be covered with McCatsup. Which reminds me. The 13-year-old said that when you buy me another pair of jeans, he'd like them a little longer. He said the last pair was so short on him that people could see my socks."

"I'll try to remember," she promises. "Meanwhile, what are you going to wear tonight?"

"Well, I suppose I could wear the tuxedo pants with an R.E.M. T-shirt."

"You can't do that," she says.

"Too casual?"

"It's my turn to wear the R.E.M. T-shirt."

Not only is my closet a great deal more active than it was before I met her, so is my mailbox. The action becomes particularly frantic as the holidays approach.

It is late October. She is sitting on the couch when I come home from work.

"Hi," she says, "how was your day?"

"Fine. How was yours?"

"Not bad. Did you check the mail on the way in?"

"Yep. Nothing but junk." I lob the junk in question toward the waste-basket. It still is in mid-air when she leaps from the couch, dives the length of the living room and makes a one-handed grab like Ozzie Smith going deep in the hole for a sinking line drive.

"You almost threw away my Horchow," she exclaims.

"Your what?"

"It's the new Horchow catalog. I've been waiting for it for weeks."

"Sorry. I had no idea you were planning to buy a new Horchow. Is our old one broken?"

"A Horchow isn't something you buy. It's the name of a company in

Dallas that sells wonderful things. I can't believe you thought their catalog was junk mail."

"To me, junk mail is anything that doesn't begin, 'Dear Sir: This is to inform you that a distant relative has passed away and left you as the majority stockholder of British Petroleum.'"

The Horchow, it turns out, is merely the first drop of what is to become a catalog flood. In the next few weeks we receive glossy brochures from every retail establishment this side of Bob's Porn Shop, our living room is beginning to look like the collection center for a Boy Scout paper drive and our mailman is wearing a truss.

"I don't mean to be judgmental," I say one afternoon, pushing aside a stack of Tiffany catalogs to make room for myself on the couch, "but this catalog thing is getting out of control. I just counted, and we have catalogs from 42 different stores in this condo. Does that tell you something?"

"Sure," she says. "It tells me that you missed the four in the upstairs bathroom."

Our conversation is interrupted by the arrival of the 11-year-old, who bursts into the room shouting, "Did the FAO Schwarz come yet?"

"It's in your brother's room," his mother informs him. "Look under the Abercrombie & Fitch."

"That's not fair. You promised me I could see it first."

"I know, but you got to see the Brigade Quartermaster first. Remember? It came the same day as the Crate and Barrel and the Bergdorf Goodman."

"Yeah, but he took the Brooks Brothers out of my dresser," the 11-year-old complains.

To a man who raised three sons whose only arguments about reading materials concerned who tore out Miss July, the whole conversation is hard to understand.

"I don't get it," I say, after the 11-year-old has left the room with a stack of Bloomingdale's under his arm. "Why is this family so hooked on catalogs?"

"Because catalogs can tell you what's hot," she explains.

"What difference does it make what's hot, when we only have an income that's lukewarm?"

"But, if you don't read the catalogs, how will you ever know what's in fashion when you go shopping?"

"Simple. You just stand in the middle of the store and wait for the blue light to start flashing."

She buries her nose in a Scully & Scully to indicate there's no point in continuing a conversation with a man who tried to buy her wedding ring from the Avon lady.

The only good thing about all these catalogs is, the way they're stacking up in the front hallway, she's never going to be able to get out of the door to go shopping.

Even though she does not share my interest in sports and I do not share her interest in shopping, we do manage to find a common activity when she decides to go back to college to pursue her master's degree in elementary education.

To be honest, I have mixed feelings about it at first.

On the one hand, I am proud of her desire to further her education, broaden her horizons, widen her vistas, lengthen her perspective and add three grand a year to her paycheck. On the other hand, most people already suspect that she's a great deal smarter than I am. When she gets her master's degree, she'll have it on sheepskin.

Still, I do my best to be supportive. On the evenings she has classes, I cook dinner for the kids. When she has papers to write, I volunteer to do the typing and editing. And when she mentions one evening that she needs assistance with an assignment, I am more than willing to help.

"What's the assignment?" I ask.

"We have to interact," she says.

"Fabulous. I'll get the wine and some candles and meet you upstairs in five minutes."

"Keep your shirt on," she says. "I'm talking about verbal interaction. The assignment is to explore our relationship. We're supposed to make lists of the things that we appreciate about each other."

"What does that have to with teaching second-graders not to stuff crayons up their noses?"

"I'm not sure," she concedes. "But it must be important. I'm positive that the American educational system would not waste my time with an assignment that is totally pointless and has absolutely no relevance to what actually happens in a classroom."

She's so cute when she's being facetious.

"Well, OK," I agree, "let's get started."

"First," she says, "you have to list one thing you appreciate about me."

"That's easy. I appreciate the fact that you bring joy to my days, passion to my nights, meaning to my existence and bliss to the very depths of my soul."

"Not bad," she says, jotting down my words.

"OK, now it's your turn," I prompt her.

She stares at her paper. I wait. She continues to stare. I continue to wait.

"Does this delay mean there are so many things you appreciate about me that you're having trouble deciding which one is the most significant?" I suggest.

"Something like that," she agrees. "Just give me a minute."

I give her a minute. Ten times.

"Well," she says, finally, "I, uh, appreciate the fact that you've stopped leaving your used tea bags on the kitchen window sill in the mornings."

"That's it?" I demand. "The best thing you can say about me is that I'm good with soggy tea bags? What about bliss? What about passion?"

"All right, all right. It makes me *passionately* happy that you don't leave your used tea bags lying on the kitchen window sill in the morning. There. Is that better?"

"Fine," I retort. "Then another I like about you is that sometimes you don't spend the *whole* evening sitting on your can talking to your dippy girlfriends on the phone."

"Dippy girlfriends? What about all those nights you waste hanging around with your drunken tennis-playing buddies?"

"You want to talk about drunken? Let's talk about that aunt of yours who stuck a straw into a bottle of Jim Beam at our wedding and . . . "

Before I can finish listing how much I appreciate her family, she stalks out of the room, storms upstairs and slams the bedroom door.

A little education can be a dangerous thing.

But not as dangerous as sharing your mate's interests.

PREFACE: CHAPTER 7

# *Our Family's Not Blended . . . It's Just Mixed Up*

"I just picked up a book I think we need to read," my wife announces one afternoon. "It's called *Siblings Without Rivalry*."

"Sounds interesting," I agree. "But I didn't realize you were into fiction."

"It's not fiction," she says.

"With a title like that, what else could it be? My guess is that it's probably the first in a series of satirical child-raising books. Take my word for it. The next one will be called *Bedtime Without Whining.* Then there'll be *Mealtimes Without Arguments.* And after that they'll follow it up with *Teen-agers Without Rock Music*."

"I'm telling you, this is a serious book," she insists. "It's written by two women who say it 'challenges the idea that constant, unpleasant conflict is natural and unavoidable.'"

"I can't believe you'd fall for a line like that. Anybody who's been a parent for more than an hour and a half knows that not only is conflict between kids natural and unavoidable, it's desirable. The minute they stop fighting with each other, they're going to turn on you."

"Why are you so cynical?"

"Because I've been there, that's why. Siblings are born to argue. On the day we brought our last kid home from the hospital, the 8-year-old looked into his crib and yelled, 'It's his turn to do the dishes!'"

"Well, I don't think it would hurt to give this book a . . . "

Our conversation is disrupted by the sound of shouting from the other room, where a brawl has erupted between a 10-year-old and a 13-year-old.

"Start reading," I urge.

She riffles through the book until she comes to Page 162: "How to Handle the Fighting." The chapter divides fighting into four levels.

"It says for Level I, which is normal bickering, the first step is to ignore it and think about your next vacation," she reads aloud.

I start thinking about my next vacation. But that inevitably gets me thinking about my last vacation, the one where I took three of them white-water rafting and they spent 200 miles in the car fighting over whose turn it was to make obscene gestures at passing truck drivers.

My warm recollections are interrupted by a scream of pain from the other room.

"Sounds like a good time to check on Level II," I suggest.

"Level II is when the situation is heating up and adult intervention might be helpful," she reads. "The first step is to acknowledge their anger. You're supposed to say, 'You two sound mad at each other.'"

I shrug and head for the other room.

"You two sound mad at each other," I say.

"I hate his guts and I'm gonna stuff him in the microwave," the 13-year-old roars.

"Urrghh," the 10-year-old says, struggling to pry the 13-year-old's fingers from around his throat.

"What's that book say about Level III?" I shout to my wife.

"You're supposed to inquire if this is a play fight or a real fight."

"I'm pretty sure it's a real fight."

"How can you tell?"

"The 10-year-old's tongue is turning black. What's Level IV?"

"'Situation definitely dangerous! Adult intervention necessary.' You're supposed to break them up and send them to their rooms."

"Sounds like good advice. Another 10 seconds and we'll be at 'Level V: Guns and Knives.'" I grab one kid with each hand, pull them apart and send them to their rooms.

When order has been restored, I head for my study to start writing a humor book that has just occurred to me. I don't have a complete outline, yet, but I have a working title:

*Parents Without Migraines.*

# CHAPTER 7

OOOOOOO

When my children were little, I prayed a lot.

"Oh, Lord," I would pray, wiping strained peas off the front of my shirt, "please hurry and make them old enough to feed themselves and I will be a happy man." My prayer was answered and eventually they became old enough to feed themselves. Twenty-eight times a day.

But that lesson was lost on me and I continued to pray.

"Dear God," I would groan, trying to straighten up after tying my 400th pair of shoelaces that day, "please get me to a time when I no longer will have to keep shoes on these tiny little feet." Once again, somebody up there listened to me and the tiny little feet grew into great big feet. Which go through six pairs of Nikes a year. At $67.50 a pair.

Still, my faith was strong and I kept at it.

"Heavenly parent," I would implore, as I emerged from the bathroom with a soaking shirt, wrinkled hands and the smell of Mr. Bubble forever in my nose, "just hasten the moment when I will never again have to kneel next to another tub and rinse shampoo out of a screaming kid's hair and I never will bug you after that."

The Lord heard my prayer, shook a pitying head and said, "Obviously not one of my smarter creations." And the next thing I knew my house was overrunneth with adolescent boys who took showers that lasted for 40 days and 40 nights.

Once they are combined into a blended family, parting the Red Sea is child's play compared to trying to get them all in and out of the shower on the same day.

The first time I have to try my hand at miracle making is on the day I wind up with tickets for six to a college basketball game. It will be the perfect opportunity for our new family to do something together.

"OK, you guys," I announce at the dinner table when the final splatter of spaghetti sauce has landed on the last Hard Rock Cafe sweatshirt, "we have to leave for the game in an hour. Between now and then, all four of you have to take showers. So you each get five minutes. Not a second more."

"What happens if somebody's not out in five minutes?" asks her 13-year-old.

"The other three guys can do whatever they want to him."

It is, I am forced to admit, the most fiendishly brilliant plan I have devised in two decades of fathering. If there is one thing that will get a kid moving, it is the knowledge that his brothers have permission to do anything they want to him.

They draw straws to see who goes first. Her 10-year-old wins. He races upstairs to the bathroom. As soon as I hear the water running, I set the timer on the stove for five minutes. When the timer starts I head toward the living room. My 15-year-old, I notice, is in the downstairs bathroom with his fingers on the toilet handle.

"When the timer goes off I'm going to start flushing," he explains. "That'll make the water hot and he'll burn to death." Great plan. Especially for a kid who hasn't flushed a toilet in three years.

I walk upstairs. The other two kids are standing in front of the bathroom door. Her 13-year-old is holding a bar of soap. My 12-year-old is holding a toaster oven plugged into a long extension cord.

"As soon as the timer goes off, I'm lobbing this baby in on him," he gloats. "He'll be a crispy critter."

"Don't you think that's a little extreme?" I say.

"You said *anything*," he replies. My 12-year-old and her 10-year-old have not gotten off to a very good start.

After five minutes, the timer sounds. The downstairs toilet flushes. From inside the kids' bathroom there is a howl. Followed by the sound of a shower curtain being ripped from its rod. Followed by the sound of a wet body landing on the floor.

I race back upstairs just in time to see my 12-year-old dropping his toaster, ripping off his clothes and bursting into the bathroom. A second later a naked 10-year-old comes sliding out of the bathroom.

"He didn't even let me dry off," her 10-year-old screams.

"Dry off on your own time," shouts my 12-year-old.

The next thing I know, I have a toilet flushing every five minutes. A torn shower curtain. A kid making a puddle in the hallway. A kid making a lake in the bathroom.

I don't know why I thought this plan was going to work.

It didn't have a prayer.

Even though the shower incident is not a promising beginning, the blending of our families is a relatively painless process. It does not turn out to be, as we feared, an extended two-way battle pitting my kids against her kids. In a year or so it is more of a four-way civil war. It no longer is a question of my kids fighting with her kids and her kids fighting with my kids. As soon as they really get to know each other, all four kids have learned to fight with each other equally, without regard to race, religion or surname.

From then on, my wife and I realize, we are pretty much like any other family.

It's us against them.

As in any family, the truest test of our parenthood is winter.

For three of the four seasons, parenthood has an escape clause. When things get too crazy in the house, you can send your kids to a wonderful place called "outside." You can, I suppose, send them outside to play in winter, too. But after eight or nine hours they tend to start scratching at the door and whining about being cold.

That's what happens at our house on a frosty winter evening when we find ourselves trapped in a condoful of sons who are tired of MTV, bored with Nintendo and unable to think of anything else to do that does not involve lethal weapons. It is obvious we are going to have to think of something for them to do. That's why parents get paid the big bucks.

There are several possibilities.

We can take them to a movie. In which case we would have to take out a second mortgage on our house tomorrow.

We can take them all skiing. In which case we would have to sell our house tomorrow.

We can tiptoe quietly out the back door and leave them alone for the evening. In which case there would be no house tomorrow.

"Maybe," suggests the housemother, "we can find something to do right here at home. Something that will keep them nice and quiet."

"Good idea," I agree. "You hold them down and I'll get the chloroform."

"I was thinking of a board game. How about if we play a game of Pictionary?"

"What's that?"

"It's a great game. You take a card with a word on it and draw pictures so your teammates can guess what it is. It can really be a lot of fun."

"Sounds like a nice quiet game," I concede.

She locates the Pictionary game and we choose teams. She and I and the 11-year-old will be on one team. The 13, 14 and 16-year-olds will be on the other team. We sit on the floor around the coffee table. There is a blaze in the fireplace. Hot buttered popcorn in a bowl. The ghost of Norman Rockwell hovers above us.

Play begins. The 14-year-old takes a card and starts to draw. I have no idea what his picture is supposed to be, but it does explain a lot about his latest grade in art class.

His teammates launch a barrage of guesses, ranging from "football field" to "submarine." None of which, it turns out, is even close. Time expires without a correct answer.

"It's a streetcar, you dummies," the 14-year-old shouts at his teammates.

"What a jerk," the 13-year-old yells back. "It doesn't look anything like a streetcar. Streetcars don't have wings."

"Those aren't wings. They're propellers."

"Propellers on a streetcar," shrieks the 11-year-old, erupting into waves of hysterical laughter. "What a moron."

"Oh yeah?" the 14-year-old yells, grabbing a piece of hot buttered popcorn and firing it across the coffee table. The popcorn hits the 11-year-old right between the eyes. Immediately he falls on the floor, clutching his forehead and screaming that he has a concussion.

"Hey, I was gonna eat that piece," bellows the 16-year-old, punching the 14-year-old in the back. The 14-year-old returns the swing, misses and knocks the popcorn bowl onto the floor. The 13-year-old dives for the spillage, arriving there just ahead of the cat.

Our quiet game of Pictionary does not seem to be turning out the way the manufacturer intended. We have two kids beating each other into insensibility. One kid fighting with a cat over spilled popcorn. Another kid rolling on the floor with a probable skull fracture.

In the midst of all this family blending, the housemother and I slip into our coats and tiptoe toward the back door. It seems like a perfect time for us to go out and play.

But it takes more than a daily brawl to discourage my wife. The only way they are going to get along, she insists, is if we "do things" together. I think she's got it backwards. I think the only way they are going to get along is if they don't see each other again until they all are collecting Social Security checks.

As usual, she wins. We go to movies together. We go to restaurants together. And the following spring, we decide to take them all to an amusement park. It probably isn't one of our smarter decisions, but then, when it comes to all-out, world-class, state-of-the-art stupidity, nature may never have spawned a dumber creature than a human being in search of diversion.

Dinosaurs had brains the size of walnuts. Horses have to be forced to leave a burning building. Our cat is so dumb he'll climb up a tree and not know how to get down.

But human beings are the only ones who go to amusement parks.

How stupid is that?

Well, let's talk about our trip.

At 10 a.m. we are loading the car. There are two adults and four kids.

The car has been designed to comfortably seat two adults and a canary. We stack the kids like firewood in the back seat and begin to drive to the amusement park. I don't know who said "life is short." Obviously it was a person who never drove to an amusement park with four kids in the back seat of a compact car.

A lifetime later we arrive at the park. We pay $3.50 to enter the parking lot. When we drive through the gate, an attendant directs us to the nearest open parking space. It is not in the same ZIP code as the entrance to the park.

A tram takes us to the entrance. We buy six tickets for a total of $126. It would have been more, but we are able to convince the turnstile attendant that the kid with the mustache really is under the age of six.

Inside the park, a vote is taken as to which ride to try first. The two adults vote for a gentle boat ride that glides through an enchanted storyland forest and delights the senses with music and color. The four boys vote for a roller coaster that climbs 42 stories into the air, hurls you down a hill at the speed of sound, whips you upside-down through two corkscrews and is guaranteed to induce nausea in a fighter pilot.

We find the end of the line for the roller coaster. The beginning of the line is not in the same area code. Two hours later we get into the roller coaster car. A minute and a half later the ride is over. We get out of the roller coaster car, wait for our stomachs to join us and head for the next ride. The next ride is a roller coaster that climbs 142 stories into the air, hurtles you down a hill at the speed of light and whips you through three corkscrews. Backwards.

We spend two more hours in line. A minute and a half riding. An hour looking for our stomachs.

By then it is time to eat. We stand in line for 45 minutes. We buy $2 worth of hot dogs and $3 worth of soft drinks. They cost us $28.90.

When we have finished eating, we take another vote to pick the next ride. We decide on a giant inner tube that bumps along an artificial river on waves high enough to capsize the QE2, while computerized nozzles spray you with enough water to put out the Chicago fire. Once again, the vote is 4-2. We find the end of the line. The beginning of the line is not in the same time zone.

After three hours of standing in line, it begins to rain. All four kids start to gripe because they are getting wet while waiting in line to go on the water ride. We stand in the rain for half an hour. The rainstorm turns into a thunderstorm. We run 15 kilometers to the nearest shelter. We stand under the shelter for an hour. Finally, the rain stops. Ten minutes later, the park closes.

We find our car and drive home. We have spent $158.40. Or, to put it another way, $79.20 per ride. We have blisters on our feet from walking. Cramps in our thighs from standing. Wet hair. Wet underwear. There is an aroma coming from the back seat that normally is found only in the vicinity of farm animals.

And, when we arrive home, the first thing we see is the dumb cat. He has spent the whole day on the couch. He is dry. He is well-fed. He is well-rested. He is grinning.

Who can blame him?

As a rule, of course, if teen-age boys have to "do things" with a parent, they would rather do it with their father than with their mother. And I know why. Mothers are smarter than fathers.

A typical mother of teen-age boys will say, "Why don't we all spend Sunday afternoon at the Art Museum? I hear they have a lovely display of pastel post-impressionists." Within five seconds the house will be filled with teen-age boys screaming, hurling and jumping out of second floor windows.

A typical father of teen-age boys, on the other gender, has been led to believe that father-son activities are required to involve a high probability of physical injury and a potential for dismemberment.

So a father will say, "How about if we go camping next weekend in the Killer Mosquito Forest? After that we can climb Frozen Corpse Mountain and drive three-wheelers at Skull Fracture Flats." Within five seconds his car will be filled with teen-age boys who do not know the meaning of the word "trepidation." Or how to spell it.

I am nothing if not a typical father. That's the only rationalization I can think of to explain why, the next time I decide to "do things" with my sons, I wind up clinging to a rubber raft on a raging river in West Virginia with a boatload of teen-age boys yelling "awesome" and a guide yelling "paddle for your lives."

Not only am I paddling for my life, I have driven six hours for the opportunity to do it. In a car full of boys competing to see who can be first to belch an entire sentence. I have spent $52 for a night in the Norman Bates Motel, where the toilets flush only on Fridays. Not to mention $78 at the only full-service restaurant in southern West Virginia, a gourmet Italian spot where the specialty of the house is ravioli with a side of grits.

And now we all are in a 16-foot raft with a guide named Jack and a rafting company owner named Barry, to whom I have written a check for $169. And as our boat shoots sideways into a rapids and heads directly toward a boulder just slightly larger than Mount Rushmore, I am doing my best to remember Barry's assurance that white-water rafting is the safest sport since chess.

"You're safer doing this than you were driving your car down here," he had assured me while he were being shuttled to the launching site. Of course, when we reached the launching site, he handed me a red helmet, a yellow life jacket and a waiver form declaring that it's not his fault if I fall out of the boat and shatter every bone in my body. None of which were necessary for the drive down here.

Another major difference between white water rafting and car driving is that, in car driving, you actually sit *inside* . In white-water rafting, you sit on the outer edge of the boat, with only your feet inside for balance, while you hold on to the oar with both hands and paddle for your life.

Violating most of the laws of probability, we miss the boulder, clear the rapids and emerge on the other side. We have passed our first test. The 16-year-old cheers triumphantly. The 14-year-old grins in satisfaction. The 13-year-old belches the first four words of the Gettysburg Address.

"That was wild," I exclaim.

"That was only a two," Jack yawns.

"What do you mean?"

"Rapids are classified from one to six according to their degree of difficulty. Six is the toughest. That was a two."

"So, what's a six?" I ask, "Niagara Falls?"

"Don't worry, there aren't any sixes on this river. But there are some real nice fives. Matter of fact, the one coming up is a real nice five."

As we approach the real nice five, I ask Jack what we should do if one or all of us falls out of the boat.

"Try not to go into any of those rocks head first," he advises. When it comes to wisdom, you just can't beat an experienced river guide.

We rocket into the real nice five. My side of the boat goes up into the air. Or the water goes down. It really doesn't matter which. Either way, I have so much trouble keeping my feet inside the boat that I have no time to paddle for my life.

"Keep paddling," Jack shouts. "You don't have your oar in the water."

"You're not the first person to tell me that," I shout back.

Again we survive the rapids and we complete the rest of the 10-mile trip without incident. I herd the kids into the car for the drive home. If we hurry, we may be able to get there in time for the last showing of the pastel post-impressionists.

Not everything we do together involves the opportunity for bigger and better broken bones, of course. Occasionally we get dressed up and go out together to *bar mitzvahs*, dinner dances and other social occasions.

The first time our entire family is invited to one of them, I am pleased. It promises to be one of the major social events of the year, at one of the most prestigious country clubs in town. Anybody who is anybody will be there. Anybody who would *like* to be anybody will be there. Dress will be formal. Black tie for men and competitive Halstons for women.

"This will be a whole new experience for my boys," I tell my wife. "They've never been to a country club. Do they have to wear tuxedos?"

"Sport coats and ties will be fine for them," she assures me.

The next day I check through their closets. My 16-year-old has the sport coat I bought him for the spring dance. My 13-year-old, on the other hand, does not own any dress clothes. It is not that I am cheap, necessarily. But it just didn't make sense to me to buy expensive clothes for a kid whose pituitary gland is on warp speed.

"The 13-year-old doesn't own any dress clothes," I tell my wife. "Can't he just go in khaki slacks and a nice sweater?"

"If he goes in khaki slacks and a sweater, people will think we're poor," she says. "You're just going to have to buy him a new outfit."

"If I have to buy him a new outfit, we *will* be poor," I respond.

The next day I take the 13-year-old to a clothing store. We start in the shoe department.

"See anything you like?" I ask him.

"These are cool," he says, picking up a pair of Air Jordans.

"We're going to be dining and dancing, not dribbling and slam dunking," I explain to him.

"What kind of shoes am I supposed to wear, then?"

"How about these?" I suggest, showing him a pair of cordovan loafers.

"Do they come in high tops?"

"No. And they don't have pumps in them, either. Oh, and while we're in this department, do you have any gray socks?"

"I have a pair of gym socks in my locker at school that probably are gray by now," he guesses.

I pay for the shoes and a pair of socks. He puts on the new shoes and we head for the pants department. A salesman helps us pick out a pair of charcoal-gray slacks.

"These are sort of expensive," I note, glancing at the price tag.

"They're 70 percent wool," the salesman says.

"I don't care if they're 70 percent mink. The way this kid's growing, they're going to be Bermuda shorts by the end of the month."

I pay for the slacks and we proceed to the sport coat department.

"How can I help you?" another salesman asks.

"You can find me a sport coat that costs less than a Stealth bomber," I tell him.

He takes a navy blue sport coat off the rack and slips it onto the 13-year-old. I step back to take a look.

"Perfect," I say.

"If you don't mind me saying so, sir, the sleeves seem a little long," the salesman says. "You can't even see his hands."

"He'll grow into it," I assure him. "He's not going to be wearing it until next weekend."

I pay for the sport coat and we plod on to accessories. By the time we have finished with shirts, belts and ties, my credit card and I both are worn out and the 13-year-old is limping. Somewhere between slacks and accessories, he has outgrown his new shoes.

Buying the clothes for the formal social event is the easy part. Getting them all ready in time is not. I'm not sure how I got the idea that by this time they should be able to dress themselves. I just sort of figured that kids who no longer wore things with puppies and clowns on them should be able to put on their own clothes.

But on the night we are dressing for our first big social event as a family, it is not quite that easy.

Between us we have four sons on the premises, two of whom have never worn anything more formal than a Bart Simpson sweatshirt. To get all of them into coats and ties at the same time is going to call for more split-second timing than a shuttle launch. If they start dressing too soon, by the time we are ready to leave at least two of their jackets will be more wrinkled than Ronald Reagan's neck. If they start dressing too late, we will never get there on time.

On Saturday evening, an hour before we are scheduled to leave, I tell them to begin dressing. The biggest stampede since the Oklahoma land rush thunders upstairs to the one available bathroom.

There are two bathrooms in our condo, but the other is occupied by my wife, who has been in there getting ready since Wednesday. For the past two days she has been having her meals sent in. By the time there is a vacancy in that bathroom, I know, it will be too late for me to shower. Not that it matters. After four teen-age boys get done draining the water heater, the only thing coming out of the shower head will be ice cubes.

I go up to our bedroom, put on a double layer of Speed Stick and start to dress. I am interrupted by a knock on the bedroom door.

"Who is it?"

"It's me," says the 16-year-old. "I need a pair of socks."

I find a pair of gray socks in my drawer and give them to him. It is just the beginning of a parade of barefoot boys. In less than five minutes, my sock drawer has been looted and, when there is yet another knock on the door, I announce, "Whoever it is, I hope you like pantyhose."

"I've got socks," says the 14-year-old. "I need a belt."

"See if this fits you," I say, handing him one of my belts. He wraps it around his waist. Three times. The kid's built like a snake.

"Just keep your hands in your pockets all night," I tell him. I close the door and begin to wrestle with the cuff links in my tuxedo shirt. The wrestling match is interrupted by another knock.

"Now what?" I snap.

"My tie's choking me to death," complains the 11-year-old.

"Choking to death is part of becoming a man," I inform him.

There is another knock.

"See if this knot in my tie is OK," calls the 16-year-old. I open the door again. The knot in his tie is roughly the size of a grapefruit. On the positive side, he doesn't have to worry about the ends of his tie hanging down unevenly. There *are* no ends hanging down.

"How does it look?" he asks.

"It looks like you have a paisley goiter," I tell him. "Try again."

I close the door. An instant later the bathroom door opens and my wife emerges for the first time in four days. She is stunning in an off-the-shoulder black dress. She looks like a Paris model. I, on the other hand, am nattily attired in black socks, Jockey shorts and a shirt whose unlinked cuffs are flapping around my wrists. I look like the village flasher.

"You're not ready yet," she observes.

"I've been sort of busy," I explain. "First there was . . ."

"Never mind, just let me help you with your cuff links," she says, shaking her head. "Honestly, I thought by the time I got to this age I would be done helping other people get dressed."

I don't know what she's complaining about. At least she only has one husband.

PREFACE: CHAPTER 8

# STEPCAT

It is a gray and gloomy day, my car is almost out of gas and there really is no good reason to go into the office when it would be just as easy to stay home and write my column. My wife is at work, the kids are at school and there will be nothing to distract me. They are ideal writing conditions. Leo Tolstoy probably wrote *War and Peace* on a day like this.

I take the phone off the hook, sit down at my typewriter with a pot of tea and a stack of writing paper and wait for the muse to be upon me. A few minutes later, something hops up onto my lap.

It is not the muse.

It is my stepcat.

I look down at him. He is smiling. Or smirking. It's hard to tell with cats.

"Get off my lap," I suggest.

Casually, he leaves my lap, hops up on the desk, walks across my typewriter keys and curls up on my stack of writing paper. I glance down at the piece of paper in my typewriter. What he has written is not bad, but he's no Erma Bombeck, either.

I pick up the cat, carry him out of the room and close the door. Before I get back to my desk, he begins to yowl. I sit down and try to ignore the yowls. It's like trying to ignore an air raid siren. I get up and open the door. The cat stands in the doorway and stares up at me as if he were trying to tell me something. Whatever it is, I don't understand. Cats are not very good at pantomime.

Perhaps, I guess, he is trying to tell me that he is hungry.

I walk downstairs and check his bowl. Sure enough, two pieces of his Kitty Krunchies are missing. There still is enough food in the bowl to give Garfield a stomachache, but this cat will not eat unless his bowl overfloweth.

I pour more food into his bowl and return to my typewriter. Two minutes later I hear a noise behind me. I turn around to look. A furry white paw is poking under the door.

"Now what?" I demand, opening the door. The cat sits in the doorway and stares up at me, but does not answer. The expression in his eyes seems to be saying that he would like some water. Then again, it could be saying, "Boy, is this guy stupid. All I have to do is stick my paw under the door and he drops whatever he's doing. The woman who lives here just ignores me until I get bored and walk away."

I head back downstairs and check his water bowl. There is approximately a gallon of water in his bowl. And two gallons on the floor around it. When you don't have to clean up after yourself, you don't worry much about table manners.

Once more, I walk upstairs to my typewriter. If nothing else, working at home is good for my cardiovascular system. Before I can reach my chair, I hear yowling from the living room. I walk back downstairs. The cat is standing at the front door. Apparently he wants to go outside. I'm not sure why. There's a litter box in the house and most of his other original factory equipment was modified by the vet years ago.

I open the door and he dashes outside to do whatever it is that impotent cats do. I return to my typewriter. Half a sentence later I hear more yowling. The cat whose only goal in life 30 seconds ago was to get outside now wants to come back in.

I get up, walk downstairs and open the door.

"All right, come on in," I say.

He sits on the front step and looks up at me, but he does not move. Maybe he doesn't want to come in, after all. Maybe he just wants to see how many times I can walk up and down the stairs before my heart explodes. Or maybe he wants me to come outside with him. I'm not sure why. Most of *my* original factory equipment has been modified, too.

We stare at each other for a while. Finally he walks slowly, insolently, through the door and trots back upstairs. I follow him. When I get upstairs I find him sitting on my chair in front of my typewriter. It could be worse. At least he's not drinking my tea.

Sighing, I turn off my typewriter, pack my briefcase and head for my car. It is obvious that I won't get any work done under these conditions.

If Tolstoy had owned a cat, *War and Peace* would have wound up as a short feature in *Reader's Digest.*

# CHAPTER 8

OOOOOOOO

All right, I'll admit it. I do not love all members of my new family equally.

And the member of my new family I love least equally is my stepcat.

I've been honest with him about it. I do not hold him on my lap and gently stroke his fur. I do not talk sweetly to him. I do not prepare him gourmet dinners and beg him to take just one bite.

It's not that I have anything against this particular cat. It's just that, like all cats, he does not seem to serve any particular purpose. I can't ride him. If I take him out into a field and throw a ball, the only thing he will do is sit and stare at me until I finally go and retrieve it for him. If I leave him at home alone, he will not protect my valuables. When I return from work, he will not bring me my slippers, fetch my newspaper or mix me a vodka and tonic.

He is, as far as I can determine, useless.

My stepcat seems to sense my negative feelings about him. And he reacts in typical cat fashion.

He clings to me.

I cannot sit down in the living room without him jumping up onto my lap. I cannot sit down at the kitchen table without him rubbing up against my shins. I cannot sit down in the smallest room in the house without seeing a small, white paw sliding under the door.

Bugging me is an all-day project for my stepcat. But mornings really bring out the animal in him.

People do not mess with me in the morning.

My wife gives me a wide berth. My stepsons avoid me. My friends do not call. Everyone knows that I am a miserable grump in the morning.

The only one who is not intimidated is my stepcat.

At night, I will close the bedroom door, slip the bolt, fasten the padlock and slide a triple dresser in front of it. When I awaken in the morning, the first thing I will see is a pair of oval green eyes staring from the pillow next to me.

"Go away," I will growl.

The oval green eyes will blink, but they will not leave.

"I don't like you," I will snarl.

The cat will move closer to my face.

"I dreamt last night that I was playing a violin and guess where the strings came from?" I will taunt.

The cat will lick my nose and purr.

No matter what I say, that cat will not get out of bed until I do.

Nothing can move him. His mother could be in the kitchen, filleting a 12-foot flounder and that cat will not leave my side. His brothers could be spilling milk until it was whisker-deep on the dining room floor and that cat will not budge.

But the instant I get out of bed, he will jump up, wrap himself around my ankle and we will walk downstairs together. And he will stay wrapped around my ankle until I open the cupboard door, take out his carton of cat treats and put a handful on the floor for him.

He and I both know I do not do this because I care for that cat. I do it because the moment I walk into the kitchen he begins to screech at the top of his furry little lungs until he makes me so crazy I will do anything to shut him up.

I'm not sure what's in those treats. According to the labels, the ones in the blue cartons are flavored with chicken, the ones in the red cartons taste like meat and the ones in the pink cartons contain tuna. My guess is that all three are full of high-grade crack.

There is nothing my stepcat, the junkie, will not do to get these treats. He will leap over a can of tuna to get to them. He will break into a cage filled with rabid pit bulldogs to get to them. He will confess his sins on Oprah Winfrey's show to get them.

When I first joined the family, he got the treats only on special occasions. His birthday. Christmas. Any time he went a whole day without bringing home half a chipmunk.

Gradually, his dependency increased. He began to demand them every morning. Whoever got up first would find him standing in front of the cupboard, screeching until he got a handful of treats. After a while, he started to screech whenever anyone walked into the kitchen, no matter what time of day it was.

Eventually he had to have them whenever anyone moved anywhere in the house. If you got up to change channels on the television, he would

sprint to the kitchen and start screeching. We spent one entire evening imprisoned on the couch watching the Shopping Channel because we were afraid to move.

But his screeching is loudest in the morning.

The first thing I want in the morning is a glass of unsweetened grapefruit juice. The first thing he wants is his treats. He will get his treats before I get my grapefruit juice. If I reach for the refrigerator door before he gets his treats, he will screech loud enough to shatter the juice glass in my hand.

But not even his morning fix will stop the screeching. On the first morning my stepcat and I are alone, I feed him his treats, pour my juice, take it into the living room and sit down to read the newspaper. Before I have finished the front page he is screeching in the kitchen again. I return to the kitchen. Apparently he wants to go outside now.

"You don't really want to go out," I tell him.

He screeches a little louder.

"It's cold outside," I inform him. "Willard Scott's toupee has frost on it."

He screeches even louder.

"It's so cold outside your whiskers will snap off," I warn him.

If he screeches any louder, he will set off the smoke alarm.

As the conversation with my stepcat continues, I realize that I am arguing with an animal whose brain is roughly the size of a piece of uncooked rice. And I am losing.

"All right, have it your way."

I jerk open the kitchen door. He sticks one paw out onto the patio, pulls it back and saunters back into the kitchen. I slam the door, return to the living room and pick up my newspaper.

Two headlines later he is screeching at the front door. I throw down my newspaper, get out of my chair, go to the front door and rip it open. The cat sits in the doorway and stares outside.

"You said you wanted to go out. So go out." Now *I* am screeching.

He smirks up at me.

Arguing with him is a waste of time, I realize. I will have to outwit him. I walk outside and stand on the sidewalk in front of the condo.

"Come on out," I urge him.

He sits in the open doorway, yawning.

"It's really not that cold," I assure him. The hairs on my legs are snapping off.

He sits in the doorway, snickering.

"I think I heard a mouse out here," I lie. What I actually hear is the sound of my furnace developing a hernia as it tries to keep the house warm against the frigid air that is blowing through the open door.

He sits in the open doorway, chortling.

I begin to make mouse sounds. In mid-squeak, a door opens and the guy who lives in the condo next to ours emerges. He is on his way to work. He is wearing a top coat and a three-piece suit. He is whistling.

I am wearing a bathrobe and goosebumps. I am squeaking. He sees me standing on the sidewalk. He sees the cat sitting in the doorway.

"If he won't let you come in, you're welcome to stay at my house," he says.

"Mind your own business," I snap. He hurries away.

I turn back to the doorway. The cat no longer is there, but I can see him through the window. He is in the living room, sleeping on my newspaper. It takes more than a grumpy man in a bathrobe and goosebumps to intimidate a cat.

To be fair about it, there are times when my stepcat has good reason to screech. During a fit of creative redecorating, for instance, my wife decides to move his litter box, which has been in the same location for the past several years.

"It's not very attractive there," she points out.

"Now that you mention it, I don't remember ever seeing a litter box on the cover of *Town and Country*," I agree. "Why don't we move it into the 13-year-old's room?"

"I don't know," she says, "it doesn't smell too good, sometimes."

"That's because he never throws his dirty laundry into the hamper. If you'd make him . . . "

"I meant the cat's box doesn't smell too good," she interrupts.

"Well, let's try it and see what happens."

I carry the cat's box into the 13-year-old's room and put it in a corner. A few hours later I am in the living room when I notice the cat walking slowly and majestically up the stairs. A minute later he comes back down the stairs. In two frantic leaps.

There is a pained expression on his face. I have seen that expression before. I have *worn* that expression before. Any father who ever has lived in a house with more teen-agers than bathrooms has worn that expression.

I walk back upstairs with the cat and tap on the 13-year-old's door.

"Who is it?" the 13-year-old demands.

"It's the cat."

"Cats can't talk," he says.

"They also can't turn doorknobs. Open up. He wants to visit his litter box."

The 13-year-old opens the door. The cat knocks him down, hurdles a pile of dirty laundry and leaps into the litter box.

After a few days, the 13-year-old decides he doesn't want the cat box in his room. He moves it into the 10-year-old's room. After a few weeks, the 10-year-old *notices* that there is a cat box in his room. He moves it back into the hall. By now the cat, who never did have much of a sense of humor, is starting to get downright surly.

Each day after that the cat box gets moved to another location. Each day, the cat's disposition gets a little nastier.

With all that moving, it's only a matter of time until the inevitable happens. I am notified that the inevitable has happened by the cat's mother one morning.

"Have you seen the cat's litter box?" she asks.

"You mean we've lost it?"

"I think it's safe to assume that nobody broke into our house overnight and stole it," she allows. "Although I guess we could call the police and have them check the pawn shops for hot litter . . . "

"Just help me look for it," I interrupt. "If that cat gets much grouchier he's going to start wearing a hockey mask and carrying an ax."

We spend an hour looking for the cat box. Although it probably seems a lot longer to the cat, who follows us from room to room making some really ugly sounds. Finally we find it. It is in the furnace room, hidden behind the water heater.

Shooting us both a nasty look, the cat picks up a magazine, walks into the furnace room and slams the door behind him.

Not that I blame him. I'd snarl, too, if I had to start my day by hunting for the bathroom.

On most days, though, I don't have much sympathy for my stepcat. Not only does he seem determined to make my life miserable, I'm starting to suspect he is trying to make it shorter.

According to a magazine article I once read, pets are supposed to be good for your heart.

"Regular contact with a pet can significantly and healthfully reduce the heart rate of Type-A people, those competitive individuals who are considered at risk for coronary heart disease," the article reported.

It must have been referring to other kinds of pets. Like dogs. Or tarantulas.

When I walked down the aisle with my stepcat's mother, my heart was strong and I was in perfect health. In a matter of months my heart had developed a nervous twitch and my wife was shopping for black dresses and veils.

Maybe I'm getting paranoid. But I am convinced that someone has taken out a huge insurance policy on my life and named that cat as the beneficiary. I'm at the point of checking under my hood every day before I start my car.

Not that he would do anything so obvious. He's too sneaky for that.

When the heart attack happens, he'll be out of town. With three witnesses.

No one will remember the way he would wait until I was just beginning to doze off on the couch and then leap onto my chest from the top of the bookcase. The coroner's report won't make any mention of the number of times he lurked under the bed until I walked by and then stuck out a paw to grab my shoestrings. Not even the most thorough autopsy will be able to measure the accumulated effect of coming home from work three days in a row and finding a mouse in the final stages of rigor mortis on the welcome mat.

One evening after dinner I mention my suspicions to the future Widow Stewart.

"I think that cat's out to get me," I tell her.

"Don't be silly," she says. "He loves you. Why do you think he always likes to be close to you in the morning when you read the newspaper?"

"He doesn't like to be *close* to me," I point out. "He likes to wait until I'm concentrating on whatever I'm reading and then jump off the top of the refrigerator and land in the middle of the sports section. I'm not sure how much more of that kind of closeness my heart can take."

"Your nerves do seem to be a litle shaky lately," she concedes. "Maybe you should start drinking de-caf."

"It's not the coffee," I insist. "It's the cat. Pets are supposed to be soothing influences. This one has done everything but sneak up behind me with a pair of cymbals. He's not going to be happy until they're probating my will."

"Why in the world would the cat want to get rid of you?"

"Are you kidding? He's resented me ever since we got married."

"Well, you two did get off to sort of a bad start," she admits. "But it's not entirely his fault. You could have been a little more diplomatic about explaining the new sleeping arrangements to him instead of just pushing him off the bed. I still think it wouldn't have hurt you to have slept on a rollaway that first night we got back from our honeymoon. You know how much he missed us while we were gone."

"How could he have missed us?" I demand. "You called him every night. Sometimes I think you would have preferred taking him on the honeymoon and leaving me at home."

"That's ridiculous," she says. "How can you be jealous of a cat?"

She gets up from the table, kisses the cat, scratches me behind the ear and goes to the living room to make a phone call.

The cat stays on the kitchen counter and watches as I start to clear off the table. I pick up a bowl of spaghetti sauce in one hand, stack two glasses and a nearly full coffee cup on the plates in the other hand and tuck half a loaf of Italian bread under my arm. As I turn toward the sink, the cat leaps four feet from the counter and lands on the floor in front of me. I also jump four feet. Straight up.

By the time I come back down, there is a broken glass on the floor, spaghetti sauce on the ceiling and a wet spot on the front of my pants. Which I'm hoping is cold coffee.

Worst of all, the cat is sitting there, smirking at me. I feel my heart pound and my blood pressure surge. There's not room enough in this house for both of us. That cat is going. Through the wall. I pull back my right foot. It's field goal time.

"Don't you dare kick that cat," a voice yells from the living room.

I was right. There *is* a plot on my life. But I'm starting to suspect that the cat is not in it alone. He may be only the hit man.

If the cat does get me, I certainly won't be his first victim. Nearly every day he prances home with a mouse, a bird or a chipmunk in his mouth. Or parts thereof. I wouldn't mind if once in a while he'd come home with a prime rib or a lobster. But it's always an animal for which I have no recipes in my cookbook.

Generally, though, he brings his catches home as victims, not guests. Except for late one night when I open the front door to let him in and notice something that looks like a twig dangling from his mouth onto his chin whiskers.

"What's that hanging out of his mouth?" asks the cat's mother.

"I don't know," I tell her. "But I'll be glad to ask him."

I rap the cat smartly behind his left ear. He opens his mouth, probably to complain about his civil rights being violated. A small, brown shape tumbles out and scurries down the hallway, dragging its twig behind it.

"What was that?" my wife screams. Like many women, she is easily frightened by rodents.

"It looks like a mouse," I say. "But it's hard to tell from here."

"Then why don't you get down off the coffee table and go look?"

"Why do I have to go look?" I demand.

"Because that's your job," she says. "You're the man."

"Thank you very much, Bella Abzug."

I get down from the coffee table and walk slowly down the hallway. I find the mouse crouched in the corner. He does not appear to be injured. On the other hand, he does not appear to be in a particularly good mood, either.

I pick up a wastebasket and approach him cautiously. My plan is that I will trap him in in the wastebasket, carry him outside and release him. Then the cat and I will have a long talk about bringing friends home for dinner without calling first.

Although it seems like a sensible plan to me, the mouse apparently disagrees. As I approach him he fakes left, cuts right and sprints to the laundry room. The last I see of him, he is disappearing under the washing machine.

"Did you get rid of him yet?" calls a voice from the living room.

"I'm going to need a little help," I admit.

"What kind of help?"

"I have to move some things out of the way so you can grab him."

"I'm not touching that mouse," she declares.

"All right, then, *you* lift the washing machine and I'll grab him."

She pokes her head into the laundry room.

"What do you think he's doing under the washing machine?" she asks.

"Probably trying on my lost socks," I guess. "Let's just lock the laundry room door and go to bed. We can catch him in the morning."

We go to bed. Just as I am drifting off to sleep she rolls over against me and I feel warm breath in my ear.

"I'm worried about him," the warm breath whispers.

"Who?" I mumble.

"The mouse. Do you think he's all right?"

"Why shouldn't he be all right? *He's* getting a good night's sleep."

"Maybe he's hungry. There's nothing in that laundry room for him to eat."

"Big deal. There's nothing in the kitchen for me to eat, either, but that doesn't keep you awake at night. Besides, I thought you hated mice."

"I do. But I don't want him to starve to death."

Having previously been married to a woman who was a first cousin to Mother Nature, I know there is only one way I am going to get any sleep on this night. I get out of bed, go to the kitchen, find a piece of cheese and slip it under the washing machine.

For the next several days she pops her head into the laundry room twice a day to chat with the mouse. Three times a day she slips wedges of brie under the washing machine, even though we're not sure if the mouse is still in there. If he is, it's probably because he's too fat to get out from under the washer. He may be too fat to get through the laundry room door.

As it turns out, we never do see the mouse again. But we do get a message from him a few weeks later. The message is relayed to me by my wife, who summons me to the kitchen. When I arrive, she is standing on a chair and pointing to an open drawer beneath the stove.

"Look in that drawer," she yells.

I look into the drawer, which is filled with dishcloths, towels, potholders, place mats, napkins and a generous supply of small, black pellets.

"What do you think those are?" she demands.

"Poppyseeds?" I guess.

"Mouse droppings," she snaps, glaring at me as if I were personally responsible for dropping them.

"So, what do you expect me to do about them?" I ask.

"Find that mouse and get it out of here."

"Let me see if I have this straight. You expect me to go into that drawer and look for a rat that is trapped, vicious and probably has some terrible disease?"

"Whatever he has, it certainly isn't constipation," she points out. "Anyway, it's not a rat. It's just a tiny mouse. So quit stalling and get rid of it. Unless you're afraid."

"I'm not afraid," I inform her. "But you can't be too careful around wild animals. What if I stick my hand in there and he bites my typing finger? Then I wouldn't be able to work and I'd lose my job and we'd have to sell all our belongings and the mortgage company would cancel our loan and we'd have to live in the car until the finance company repo . . . "

"Oh for goodness sake," she interrupts, "it's only a mouse. And the way you're fooling around, it's going to die of old age before you do anything about it."

"You don't understand," I explain. "I don't like rodents. When I was little, I used to cover my eyes during *Tom and Jerry* cartoons. I was the only boy in junior high who didn't rush home after school to watch the *Mickey Mouse Club*. I never got to see Annette's T-shirt grow up."

"Well, if you don't do something, you're never going to eat again," she warns. "Either get that mouse out of here or I'm not cooking another meal in this kitchen."

I hate it when she gives me tough choices like that. But she has me between a rock and a burnt place.

Cautiously, I approach the open drawer, reach in and pull out a dishrag.

"Well, that's that," I tell her, "looks like he's not here anymore."

"Keep looking," she says. "He's probably at the bottom of the pile."

One by one I pull out dishrags, towels, potholders and napkins. Eventually the drawer is empty. There is no mouse in sight. I resume breathing.

It's not that I was afraid, exactly. But if that mouse had still been in there, I know what we would have done. We wouldn't have killed it. We wouldn't have thrown it out. We wouldn't even have spoken harshly to it about its toilet habits.

We would have kept it as a pet. Even though we have these two rules at our house about pets.

Her rule is that our family will not accept into membership any pet that cannot fix its own breakfast. It is a rule that went into effect before we met, four days after her youngest kid swore that if she let him get a guinea pig, he'd feed it 10 times a day and clean its cage every hour on the hour.

My rule is that we're never again going to get a pet that cannot be flushed. It's a rule that goes into effect on the day the guinea pig dies.

I am informed by my wife of the guinea pig's demise on a Sunday night.

"Well," I say, "it could be worse. The garbage pickup is Wednesday."

"What are you saying?"

"I'm saying that if we had to wait much longer than that, things could get pretty rank around here."

"You don't mean you intend to throw that poor thing into the garbage?"

"Actually, *I was* sort of saying that," I admit. "Unless there's reason to believe he was registered for an organ donor program and there's a long list of people waiting to receive his kidneys. I suppose we could look on the back of his driver's license and check it out."

"How can you be so heartless?" she sniffles. "He was so sweet and cute."

"Sweet and cute? You said a million times you couldn't stand that thing. The only reason he lasted as long as he did was because you couldn't find a hit man who specialized in small animals."

"Maybe. But you can't just toss him in the garbage. He was a living thing."

"So? You want us to sit *shiva* ?"

"Of course not. But I want him to have a proper burial."

"No problem. First thing in the morning I'll call Arlington National. Do you happen to know if he fought in any foreign wars? I don't think we'd be able to get Billy Graham for the eulogy, but Jim Bakker probably isn't doing anything right . . . "

"If you're going to be like that, let's just drop the whole subject," she snaps. Which is her way of saying that she will have a headache tonight. And probably every night until that guinea pig is lying under a granite marker.

On Monday morning after she leaves for work I carry the guinea pig outside to find a suitable final resting spot. The spot I select is shaded by a small tree. I start to dig. Two inches beneath the surface I hit a root. I will have to find another spot.

I dig in another spot a little further from the tree. The root in this spot is three inches beneath the surface. In the next half hour I try 17 different spots and discover that the little tree has more roots than Alex Haley.

Eventually I have a hole. I put the guinea pig into it. The hole isn't deep enough. I take him out and dig some more. After another 15 minutes I try the hole for size again. Still not deep enough. After another hour of digging, the truth dawns on me. While I am digging, the guinea pig is expanding.

Finally I have a hole that is deep enough. I put the guinea pig in the hole and cover him with dirt. I am back in the house, washing my hands, when the phone rings. It is the deceased's grandmother.

"Did you bury him?" she asks.

"I buried him."

"I appreciate it," she says. "What kind of box did you put him in?"

"Box?"

"You did put him in a shoe box, or something, didn't you? You certainly didn't just put him in the ground and cover him with dirt."

"What kind of a heartless brute do you think I am?" I demand.

She hangs up. I go upstairs to her closet to get a shoe box.

I return to the grave, exhume the guinea pig, put him in the box and realize that now the hole is going to have to be twice as big. I dig for another hour, put the box in the hole, stomp on it a few times and cover it with dirt. I have shot an entire morning burying a guinea pig. My back aches from shoveling. My fingernails are cracked from pulling rocks out of the ground. And, the worst part of it is, my troubles may not be over. On the day after the funeral, her kid starts campaigning for a pony.

# JOINT CUSTODY

There are two kinds of parents.

There are parents who swear that every moment they spend with their kids is a priceless gem to be stored forever in their bank vault of memories.

And then there are honest parents.

Honest parents are the ones who admit they could survive an hour or two without phones ringing, TVs blasting and refrigerator doors hanging open. They're the ones for whom the patter of little feet is starting to sound like an endless stampede.

Honest parents love their children, too. But they're not trying to kid anybody. There are times when they would trade an internal organ for 20 minutes of peace and quiet.

No parents are more aware of the difference kids make around the house than those who share custody of their children.

On the days the children are at their "other" parent's house, there is food in the refrigerator and privacy in the bathroom. Those are the days when entire conversations can be completed without interruption and entire television programs can be viewed without a voice whining, "This show rots big time. Let's switch to MTV."

For those parents, the most difficult time is the hour before the kids show up. Also known as "the calm before the demolition derby."

Saturday mornings are our calm.

The television screen stares silently into a living room in which there are no empty tennis shoes, Nintendo games or couch cushions on the floor. The telephone is sleeping peacefully. The toilet seat is down. The leftovers from a civilized breakfast for two are stored in the refrigerator.

"Why are you so quiet?" my wife usually will ask.

"I was just wondering how long it will be before we have another meal without round-robin arguments, burping symphonies and contests to see who can be the first to suck his mashed potatoes through a straw."

"I thought you missed having the kids here."

"Of course I do. But after a week in the adult world, it takes awhile to adjust to the return of the barbarians."

"I understand," she will say, patting my hand. "It *was* nice going a whole week without a *Police Academy* movie."

"Not to mention a week without having to settle an argument about who hid the leftover fried chicken under the couch so his brothers wouldn't eat it."

"A week without the water turning stone cold 10 seconds after you get into the shower."

"A week without Dorito crumbs in the carpet."

"A week without . . . "

Our pleasant reminiscences will be interrupted by the sound of the front door crashing open, indicating that either the first of the kids has arrived or we are being raided by the LAPD.

The kid will head immediately for the living room, where he will simultaneously turn on the television, the stereo and the Nintendo game. The next kid through the door will sprint to the kitchen, where he will clear everything off the top three shelves of the refrigerator and make a sandwich. The kid after him will race from room to room, turning on every light he can find.

"How long are they going to be here?" I will shout over the din.

"One hundred and sixty-eight hours," she will shout back. "But who's counting?"

It's not that we look forward to the days when the kids are not at our house. It's just that we hate to deprive their "other" parents of all that pleasure.

Honest.

# Chapter 9

OOOOOOOOO

There are a lot of good things to be said about joint custody.

Of course, most of them are being said by people who don't *have* joint custody.

Parents who have been there for any length of time know that there is one iron-clad, written-in-stone, never-to-be-broken-or-even-bent rule that applies to every child who ever has split time between households:

*Whatever they can't live without is at the other parent's house.*

There is no way to avoid "the other house" syndrome.

If you buy your kid two entire wardrobes — one for your house and one for the other parent's house — both of them will wind up at the other parent's house. It doesn't matter if you buy toothbrushes by the gross, they will never have one in the bathroom at your house.

I'm not sure how my stepsons do this. Or when.

All I know is that on Saturday afternoon, when they come to stay with us, everything they need is at their father's house. On the following Saturday afternoon, when they return to their father's house, everything they need is at our house. I think they have it all sent Federal Express from one house to the other when we're not looking.

It does no good to nag. I try that every other Saturday.

"Are you sure you have everything you need?" I will ask, as they get into my car.

They will swear that they have packed everything in their duffel bags.

We will drive home.

Thirty seconds before their bedtime they will discover that they packed everything but their books, their clothes, their guitars, their contact lenses and the science projects that are due first period Monday morning.

In desperation, I have considered hooking a chain to their father's front door and towing his entire house to our place. But I know it wouldn't help. One of them would discover that his only clean pair of underwear is back in their father's garage.

Joint custody may or may not be a good thing for kids. I'm not qualified to comment on that. But I do know one thing for sure: Joint custody will kill your car.

My car starts to feel the effects of joint custody on the first Saturday of our marriage.

"I have to go into work today," their mother informs me. "Would you mind picking up the kids from their father's?"

"Of course not," I say. I get into my car and drive to their father's, who lives a mere two time zones away. The kids come out of their father's house carrying some books and clothes.

"Got everything you need for next week?" I ask as they get into the car.

They nod their heads.

If they had been my sons, I wouldn't have trusted the sounds of those nods. But that's only because my sons have memories the size of gnats and have been in a mental fog since shortly after they learned how to walk. Everytime I pick them up at their mother's for the weekend, they manage to forget something. Her sons, I figure, can't be that spaced out.

"OK, you guys," I say when we get home, "hang your clothes in your rooms. And, if you have homework to do, get started on it now." When you're a new stepfather, it's important to establish right away who's in charge.

Three minutes later the 10-year-old appears in the living room and turns on the television.

"Homework all finished?" I inquire.

"I can't do my history homework," he says.

"Sure you can," I encourage him. "You're a very intelligent young man and I'm sure if you just sit down and concentrate for a few minutes you'll discover that, not only can you do it, you'll actually gain satisfaction from the experience of learning."

"I left my books at my dad's."

"Why didn't you just say that in the first place?"

"It's not polite to interrupt."

"I could have sworn I heard you nod when we were in front of your dad's house and I asked if you had everything you needed," I point out.

"You asked if I had everything I needed for *next week,*" he replies. "I need the history books today."

It is, I realize, probably all my fault for not asking more specific questions. Especially with a kid who could find loopholes in the Ten Commandments.

We get into the car and return to his dad's, pick up his history books and drive home. The carburetor still is crackling when the 13-year-old appears in the living room.

"I can't do my homework," he says.

"Let me guess. You left it at your dad's." I am not about to waste another perfectly good inspirational speech.

"Nope. I have it all here."

"That's good. So what's the problem?"

"I left my contact lenses at my dad's."

I return to the car and drive to his dad's for the third time that day. Which, I soon discover, makes it a slow day. In the first four weeks my car and I are involved in joint custody, we average 3.6 trips per day to their dad's, put 10,000 new miles on our odometer and see their dad more often than we see their mother.

There is a good side to it, though. At least my car and I learn right away that stepfatherhood is not much different than regular fatherhood.

Even when they do remember their stuff, joint custody guarantees a lifetime of schizophrenia for their parents.

When the kids are with their "other" parent, life is calm and orderly. The bathroom door is almost always open and the front door is almost always closed. Footprints do not appear on the furniture. Fingerprints do not appear on the ceiling. Entire sentences can be spoken without interruption.

But the biggest difference is in the kitchen.

When they are at their "other" parent's, a bag of groceries will last all week. On a week without kids, a hot dog can be dinner for two. And there will be leftovers.

All of that changes when the kids arrive. They come through the front door with their teeth gnashing, prepared to eat everything in their path. They are not children. They are locusts in tennis shoes.

Every other week it is the same.

On Friday, in preparation for the invasion of the teen-agers, I cash in a CD and go to the grocery store, where I empty three shelves and fill five carts.

On Saturday morning, I pick up my stepsons at their father's. When we get home, the 13-year-old drops his coat in the hallway, lobs his duffel bag onto the couch and walks out of his shoes en route to the kitchen. I hear the refrigerator door open. A few seconds later, a voice calls from the kitchen:

"When are you going to the store?" the voice asks.

"I went to the store yesterday," I inform it.

"There's nothing in here to eat," the voice replies.

While I am pondering how $134.63 can buy nothing to eat, a car pulls up in front of the house and drops off *my* kids for the weekend. The 12-

year-old comes in first.

"Hi, nice to see . . ." I begin.

"When are you going to the store?" he interrupts.

"I went to the store yesterday," I reply.

"There's nothing here to eat," he says.

"How do you know? You haven't even been to the kitchen yet."

"There's *never* anything to eat here."

The 12-year-old lobs his gym bag on top of the 13-year-old's duffel bag and heads for the kitchen.

The front door opens and the 15-year-old thunders in.

"Hi, nice to see . . ." he begins.

"I went to the store yesterday," I snap.

He shrugs his shoulders, adds his gym bag to the collection on the couch and heads for the kitchen.

An hour later the kitchen is empty. So is the refrigerator, the cupboard, the bread box, the cookie jar and the cat's dish.

I start to fix dinner. The menu for tonight is meat loaf and mashed potatoes. The meat loaf recipe calls for a cup of catsup. I search through the refrigerator and the cupboards.

"Where's the catsup?" I ask my wife. "I just bought a quart of it."

"Your 12-year-old finished it at lunch," she says.

"What could he possibly have had that he put a quart of catsup on?" I ask.

"He didn't put it *on* anything. He drank it."

I substitute Bloody Mary mix for the catsup and finish cooking. When everything is ready, I call them to dinner and carry the meat loaf to the table.

"Cool," exclaims the 15-year-old. "A hamburger."

"It's a meat loaf," I reply, impaling his sleeve with a serving fork to keep him from putting dinner for six between two pieces of bread.

"Why didn't you make a bigger one?" demands the 13-year-old.

"I used the biggest roasting pan I could find," I inform him. "You want a meat loaf any bigger than this, you're going to have to figure a way to fit the bathtub into the oven."

Dinner, which took three hours to prepare, disappears in 17.3 seconds.

I go directly to bed to rest up for Sunday morning, when I will make breakfast: a side of bacon, a grove of orange juice, a platter of pancakes big enough to give Aunt Jemima a slipped disk, a tanker of . . .

# RECYCLED ROMANCE

All the world may love a lover, but it doesn't seem to know just how to react to recycled newlyweds.

If your skin is smooth, your stomach flat and your memory goes back no further than Billy Carter, you can get away with just about anything in the name of love. You can hug in public. You can kiss in public. You can walk down the street with your hands groping in each other's hip pockets.

The world can't get enough of young love. I once saw a couple barely past adolescence consummate their marriage during the first dance at their wedding reception. The mother of the bride wiped away a tear and gushed, "Aren't they precious?"

It's different when you're circling the track for the second time. As I begin to understand one afternoon when I am having dinner with my bride and a few of our friends. In the middle of the meal, a guy on the other side of the table looks at me and says, "Aw, man, do you two *have* to do that stuff in public?"

"Do what stuff?" I ask.

"You know, all that gushy stuff."

"All we're doing is holding hands," I protest.

"That's what I mean," he says. "At your age, it looks ridiculous."

"What do you mean, at our age? We're not exactly ready to go live on a golden pond."

"I know that," he says. "But that kind of stuff is for kids. Besides, I don't know why you'd want to do it, anyway. You're already married."

"I know we're married," I reply. "That's what the judge just got done telling us an hour and a half ago. Not only that, we thought we'd risk worldwide ridicule by going on a honeymoon. She even bought an orthopedic peignoir for the event."

Seven months later, we still hold hands, but we no longer are surgically joined at the palms. Our relationship has matured. But not enough, apparently, to suit society. As I discover on the day I walk through the office with a bouquet of roses in my hand.

"What's with the flowers?" a co-worker asks.

"They're for my wife," I explain. "It's our anniversary."

"Oh yeah? Which one?"

"The current one."

"I didn't mean which wife. I meant, which anniversary?"

"Oh. It's our seventh."

"Well, congratula . . . hey, wait a minute. How can it be your seventh anniversary? You just got married last August and this is only March."

"That's what I meant. It's our seven-month anniversary. Every month we celebrate with flowers or dinner or something."

"You're kidding," my co-worker snickers. "You don't actually celebrate monthly anniversaries."

"Sure we do."

"What other kind of stuff do you do?" she asks. "Do you wear her ring on a chain around your neck? Does she sleep in your letter sweater?" As I walk away from her desk, she is convulsed with laughter.

Like a lot of the rest of the world, she has bought the idea that there is an age limit for gushy stuff. A statute of limitations on romance. And perhaps she is right. Maybe all of this gushy stuff is merely honeymoon hangover and one day soon we will wake up and act our age.

But I certainly hope not.

Because the world has it all wrong. This gushy stuff isn't something that should be entrusted only to the young. Young lovers take it too much for granted. They assume it will last forever. That it is indestructible, requiring no effort and no care.

Those of us who have been recycled know better.

# CHAPTER 10

OOOOOOOOOO

The problem with real life is that reality keeps sneaking into it.

In real life, goodness does not always triumph over evil, couples do not necessarily live happily ever after and you can't count on your full purchase price being cheerfully refunded if you are not completely satisified.

And, sometimes, anniversaries do not go exactly as planned.

As our first anniversary approached, I spent a great deal of time thinking about how we should observe it.

We could shoot all the works and fly to England for a dazzling weekend of sightseeing and shopping. We could shoot some of the works and fly to New York City for an exciting weekend of theater and dining. We could keep our works in the bank and spend the night in our condo eating Chinese carryout and watching a *Taxi* rerun.

Whatever we did, I promised myself, it would be romantic, with candles and wine and hand-holding and sweet murmurs. And occasional heavy breathing.

A few weeks before the anniversary, I bring up the subject.

"How do you think we should celebrate our first anniversary?" I ask the woman whose heavy breathing I'd most like to hear.

"I know exactly how we're going to celebrate it," she replies. "We're going to be at my sister's wedding. She's getting married in Atlanta the day before our anniversary."

"Well, that's not bad. We can drive down for the wedding and then spend our anniversary taking a leisurely drive home. Just the two of us. Maybe we can stop at some secluded little . . . "

"Four of us," she points out. "We have to take my boys with us. After all, it *is* their aunt getting married."

We drive to Atlanta for her sister's wedding. Two days later, on our first anniversary, we pack the car and head for home with the kids in the backseat. Seated directly behind me is the 14-year-old. As we pull away from the reception, he takes out his cassette player, flips a headset over his ears and drifts off to a world inhabited exclusively by teen-agers. Before we get to the Interstate, I hear a whining sound behind me. I'm hoping it's the Georgia State Patrol. But I know better. It's the 11-year-old.

"What's the problem back here?" I ask.

"His music is making me deaf," the 11-year-old complains.

"How can you hear his music when he's wearing a headset?" I wonder.

"It's leaking out of his nose."

Our first anniversary is not turning out the way I had hoped, but at least we are together and she is in the seat next to me. I reach across to take her hand. Our fingers touch. They intertwine. Just as they are about to start breathing heavily, a voice from the backseat shouts, "I think I'm going to hurl."

I glance into the rearview mirror. The threat is coming from the 14-year-old, who is shouting because he has forgotten to take off his headset.

"Why are you going to hurl?" I ask.

"Riding in the backseat makes me carsick sometimes," he shouts.

I look at his mother.

"It's up to you," she shrugs. "You're the one sitting directly in front of him."

I pull the car to the side of the road. The 14-year-old and his mother trade places. We drive some more. Just inside the Tennessee border, the 11-year-old notices the fireworks outlets. In Tennessee, there are fireworks outlets approximately every 20 yards along the Interstate and they have names like "Crazy Eddie's" and "Weird Harold's."

"FIREWORKS!" the 11-year-old shrieks, loudly enough to make *me* hurl. "We've *gotta* stop and buy some."

He shrieks for the next 50 miles before I give up and pull into a place called "Psychotic Marvin's," which sells fireworks, smoked hams and glow-in-the-dark portraits of Conway Twitty. The 11-year-old races through the store picking out fireworks like a demented Middle East arms dealer.

Finally we are back on the road again.

I spend the next six hours of our anniversary seated next to a queasy 14-year-old who has Jimmy Buffett coming out of his nose. In the backseat is an 11-year-old holding enough fireworks in his lap to blow up Beirut. And, if I adjust the rearview mirror just right, I can see my wife, who has been sleeping since Knoxville.

There's entirely too much reality in my life.

But reality is an immediate and inescapable part of second marriages.

In first marriages, there is an introduction, an interlude, a time to get to know each other.

With second marriages, the wedding may have to be squeezed in between a soccer practice and a school play. On the way to the wedding night after a second marriage, there's a good chance you'll have to drop off the kids at their dad's. First honeymoons can be ruined by canceled flights and lost luggage. The biggest threat to second marriage honeymoons are chicken pox and ear infections.

Unlike chicken pox, kids do not clear up after a week or so. They just keep breaking out. The trick is to guess when. Because, when you're drawing up a list of the great oxymorons of our time, it has to start with "family planning." Like "jumbo shrimp" and "plastic glass," "family planning" is a phrase that contradicts itself.

You may be able to plan how many kids you're going to have and when you're going to have them. But, once they show up, you can forget any family plan that involves events more than 10 minutes into the future.

You think you're going to the Bahamas next weekend for a romantic getaway? Don't even bother to pack. When you have one hand on your passport and the other on the front doorknob, at least one kid will come down with a temperature of 103.

After waiting six months, you finally got tickets to see *Miss Saigon*? Give them to the childless couple next door. Because that's the night your youngest kid will be making her debut as the third daffodil from the left in the fourth-grade production of the spring play.

It doesn't get any better with age.

On a Saturday when our teen-agers all had iron-clad plans to spend the night at friends' houses, we decided to stay home and follow the advice of a magazine article that suggested moving the romance into the living room once in a while. We set the stage with soft music, candlelight, chilled wine, silk pajamas and a blanket on the floor. Somewhere between the second and third pajama buttons, the front door burst open and my 13-year-old thundered in. Leading his basketball team.

Parents who have been in the business for a while know that planning something as simple as a family meal generally is a waste of brain cells. To parents, *Guess Who's Coming To Dinner?* is not just a movie title, it's a daily question.

I don't remember dinner being optional when I was a kid.

The way I remember it, attendance at the dinner table was mandatory. Any kid who missed it was considered AWOL and could be shot on sight as a deserter. The only exception I can recall was on Sept. 7, 1963.

"Looks like I won't be here for dinner tonight," I informed my mother.

"Why not?" she demanded.

"Mom, I'm getting married this afternoon. Don't tell me you forgot about it."

"I didn't forget about it. But the wedding's at 1:30. Dinner's not until 6. Just what do you have to do that's so important you can't make it home by then?"

"We'll probably think of something."

We did think of something. But I spent most of it feeling guilty about the empty chair at my parents' table.

Our combined kids don't seem to take mealtimes that seriously. The last time I tried to pin them down about dinner I got a semi-firm commitment from the 11-year-old, an "I'll get back to you on that" from the 13-year-old and an "I'll have my people call your people" from the 15-year-old.

I call the 16-year-old, who is at his girlfriend's house. The 16-year-old *always* is at his girlfriend's house. His girlfriend's father and I are going to have a terrific argument in April about who gets to claim him as a tax deduction.

"Are you two going to be here for dinner tonight?" I ask him.

"Uh, I can't really say right now," he hedges. "Perhaps we will, but it's possible that we might not if something comes along that I'm not exactly sure about at the present moment."

"I've heard politicians take firmer positions than that on the abortion issue," I point out. "What, exactly, are you saying?"

"Maybe."

I thank him for his helpfulness and call the 21-year-old.

"We're trying to plan tonight's menu at Stewart's Diner," I inform him. "Would you care to make reservations for you and your girlfriend?"

"I'm studying for finals today," he says. "But maybe I could take a break. Can we eat between 6 and 6:15?"

"How about if I just install a drive-through window on the side of the condo?"

"That'll work."

Not only do we seldom know how many kids are going to be there for dinner, now that some of them are dating we frequently aren't sure how many of them we will recognize. I lead the league in passing bowls of mashed potatoes to teen-age girls named Missy whom I have never seen before.

But we keep trying, anyway, on the off chance that just once the number of plates and the number of people will come out even.

It never does.

Most meals turn out like they do one typical Friday when all four of our resident kids swear they are going to be home for dinner. So I go to the store, buy a roast big enough to feed them, strap it to the top of the car and drive home. As I walk into the house, a blur carrying a backpack passes me.

"Who is it and where are you going?" I ask the blur.

"It's me," the blur replies. "I'm spending the night at Graham's house. See ya."

I walk to the kitchen, where the 16-year-old is on the phone.

"Check out this roast," I say to him when he hangs up.

"Save me some," he replies. "I just made up with my girlfriend and we're going out for pizza."

I put the roast on the chopping block, cut it down the center and put one half into the freezer. A minute later, the 13-year-old appears.

"What's for dinner?" he asks.

"Is that a rhetorical question or do you actually plan to be here?"

"I was just wondering if Mark could eat with us."

I pull the other half of the roast back out of the freezer. As I am removing the aluminum foil, the 11-year-old appears in the kitchen and announces: "I'm ready to leave."

"Leave?" I ask.

"Yeah, for John's birthday party. It starts in 15 minutes and we've got to stop and buy a present on the way over there."

I chuck half the roast back into the freezer, drive the 11-year-old to the nearest toy store, grab the first present I see and drive to John's house, with one hand on the wheel and the other taping gift paper to a Baby Tears.

When I get back home, my wife is in the kitchen wrapping the other half of the roast in foil.

"Why are you wrapping the roast?" I ask.

"We don't need it," she says. "The 13-year-old just got a better offer. He won't be home for dinner, either."

I think about that for a moment.

"That means we're going to be all alone tonight," I point out. "What do you think we should do?"

"Well, there's a candle in the desk drawer, wine in the refrigerator and a blanket in the closet," she says.

If we hurry, I might be able to get to the fourth button this time before the first kid shows up.

But I wouldn't count on it. When you're a parent, the only thing you *can* count on is that your weekend will not belong to you. No one knows who first said "Thank God it's Friday." But I'm willing to bet next week's aspirin bill that it wasn't anybody with kids.

According to the results of a survey I read once, most people wind up more tired at the end of the weekend than when they started. The poll of 1,008 adults produced this analysis of how the hours are spent by a typical adult on a typical weekend:

- Housecleaning, 2 1/4 hours.

- Cooking, 2 hours.
- Laundry, $1\,^{1}/_{3}$ hours.
- Home repairs, $1\,^{1}/_{4}$ hours.
- Shopping, 1 hour.

But that's for normal people. For parents, weekends aren't that relaxing. Parents, the survey found, spent 66 percent more time cleaning, 43 percent more time cooking and 52 percent more time doing laundry than people without kids.

The pollsters didn't break down in detail how the hours of a typical parent are spent on a weekend. Probably because they couldn't find a parent who had time to fill out the questionnaire. If they had, I suspect their findings would come out pretty much the same as the poll of two adults I took at our house. According to my survey, here's how we spend the 48 hours between 6 p.m. Friday and 6 p.m. Sunday:

- Grocery shopping, 6 hours.
- Listening to four kids whining, "There's nothing in this house to eat," 6 hours.
- Laundry, 8 hours.
- Listening to four kids insisting, "I can't go to Sunday school; I don't have anything to wear," 4 hours.
- Listening to a 13-year-old complaining, "There's nothing to do around here. You've got to drive us to the Video Shack to rent some tapes," $1\,^{1}/_{4}$ hours.
- Arguing with a 13-year-old in Video Shack about whether or not *Blood Sucking Psychos from Hell* received two thumbs up from Siskel and Ebert, $1\,^{1}/_{2}$ hours.
- Watching *Blood Sucking Psychos from Hell,* $1\,^{3}/_{4}$ hours.
- Answering questions, 1 hour.
- Answering door bells, 2 hours.
- Answering phone calls, 3 hours.
- Answering phone calls that are for one of us, 0 hours.
- Reminding the 15-year-old that he has a book report due on Monday morning, $2\,^{1}/_{2}$ hours.
- Writing the 15-year-old's book report while he watches television Sunday evening, 3 hours.
- Reminding the 11-year-old that it's his turn to do the dinner dishes, 2 hours.
- Doing the dinner dishes ourselves, $^{1}/_{4}$ hour.
- Refereeing an argument between the 16-year-old and the 13-year-old about whose turn it is to play Jubangi Warrior on the Nintendo set by reminding them that they're not children anymore and they'll just have to settle it like adults, 2 hours.
- Ministering to the 13-year-old's split lip, $^{1}/_{2}$ hour.
- Cooking meals, 7 hours.
- Eating meals, 7 minutes.

• Time spent declaring to four kids that their parents want to be alone for a little while and that the first kid who knocks on the bedroom door will spend the rest of his life in an orphanage, $^{1}/_{4}$ hour.

• Time spent alone before the first kid knocks on the bedroom door, 3 minutes.

In a 48-hour weekend, that comes to 49 hours and 10 minutes. Which probably explains the "Thank God It's Monday" bumper sticker my wife has on her car.

It's hard to say when our lives began to revolve around our kids' demands. But I know it wasn't always that way. As nearly as I can remember, my childhood revolved around my parents. Dinner time was determined by when my father came home from work. Trips to the store happened when my mother could work them into her day. Whether or not I got to go to the movies was decided by whether or not one of them could find the time to drive me there. I looked forward to the day when I would be able to control my own clock.

I still am.

Not only do I not control my own clock, I do not know where my clock is. And I don't have time to look for it, because I'm too busy trying to keep up with my kids' schedules.

I have no idea how it got that way. All I know is that, if I needed open heart surgery, the operation would have to wait until the end of the 13-year-old's basketball season. If I had an appendicitis attack, I might be able to find time for an ambulance ride to the hospital. But it would have to be between the 11-year-old's Hebrew class and the 15-year-old's guitar lesson.

When you're a parent, you may own your own home, your own car and your own riding lawn mower. But you do not own your own time. You only get to borrow it until the phone rings and you hear, "Dad, I need you to take me to . . ."

For example, there is the Monday morning on which I plan to go to the office, play two sets of tennis after work, go home, eat dinner and spend a relaxing evening watching television. It will be, I tell myself, an uncomplicated day.

As I am dressing to begin my uncomplicated day, the phone rings. It is my 21-year-old, the one who decided a year ago that he was a grown man now and that he no longer had any need for parents who were always telling him what to do.

"Dad, I need you to take me to work."

"Well, I was just getting ready to go to the office."

"That's okay," he says. "Forget it. I'll just call into work and say I can't make it. They'll probably understand. I don't think they'll fire me for missing one day. And, if they do, I can always pack my guitar and move in with you guys until . . ."

"I'll be there in 15 minutes."

I drive the 21-year-old to work. Which gets me to the office an hour later than I had planned. But I still have time to get most of my work done before my tennis match.

Shortly before lunch, the phone rings.

"Sweetheart, I need you to drive the 11-year-old to Hebrew class after school," my wife informs me.

"Well, I was planning to . . ."

"I'd take him, but I have a meeting after work and then I have to take the 15-year-old to guitar practice."

I agree to take the 11-year-old to his Hebrew class. Which means that, even if I skip lunch, my two sets of tennis will have to be trimmed to one set.

I eat a vending machine sandwich while I work at my desk. The gas pains are just starting to subside when the phone rings. It is the 13-year-old.

"Did Mom tell you about the basketball game?" he asks.

"I don't think so."

"Well, we've got a makeup game this afternoon. Will you be able to get there?"

"Actually, I was planning to . . ."

"That's okay, don't worry about it, Dad. The stands will probably be real full anyway because everybody else's parents will be there."

I assure him that I will be at the game. Which means that my one set of tennis has been reduced to one backhand. I call my tennis opponent and advise him that I won't be able to play.

"How am I supposed to get a substitute at this hour?" he demands.

"Well, the 11-year-old might be able to make it after his Hebrew class," I suggest.

My tennis opponent, a bachelor with no sense of humor, slams down the phone. He obviously doesn't understand what fatherhood is all about. But then, how could he? He's never had kids. He has no way of knowing that a father's worth is measured by his response time.

That's what fatherhood is all about.

Being there.

Ever since juvenile delinquency was invented by Bill Haley and the Comets, the experts have agreed that fathers not being there probably was the underlying cause.

Kids in the '50s grew long, greasy hair and wore tight blue jeans because their fathers were too busy for them, sociologists declared.

Kids in the '60s grew hair down to their shoulders and wore love beads because their fathers were spending too much time at the country club, psychologists announced.

Kids in the '70s shaved their heads and wore safety pins in their nostrils because their fathers were spending too much time at the office, psychiatrists warned.

Having heard all these alarms, I became acutely aware of the importance of finding time to spend with my children. So I dropped my membership at the country club and cut down my time at the office. My golf handicap went up and my salary went down, but it was worth it to prevent my kids from sticking safety pins in their noses.

As they got older, though, I noticed that my problem no longer was finding time to spend with my kids. The problem was finding my kids. Just because you have to be there for a kid does not mean a kid has to be there for you.

One evening I decide to take my three sons out for dinner at a local steakhouse. It will be a men's night out. Just me and my boys. We will talk about football and about cars, about life and about sex. I will answer their questions about football and cars. They will answer my questions about life and sex.

I call the 21-year-old first.

"How about dinner Tuesday night?" I suggest. "Just you and me and your brothers."

"That's a great idea," he says. "But Tuesday's no good. I've got to study for mid-terms. How about Thursday?"

"Thursday's fine," I agree. I drive to the 13-year-old's basketball practice and pick him up.

"How about dinner Thursday night?" I say. "Just you and me and your brothers."

"I've got a game Thursday night," he says. "How about a week from Wednesday?"

"I suppose that's okay," I concede. I drive him to his mother's house. When we pull up, the 16-year-old is in the driveway, re-attaching the muffler to his car with a coat hanger.

"How about dinner a week from Wednesday?" I ask him. "Just you and me and your brothers."

"I've got weight lifting on Wednesdays," he says. "How about two weeks from Monday?"

"Well, if that's the best we can do," I sigh. I call the 21-year-old again.

"Your brothers can't make it until two weeks from Monday," I inform him. "How's that for you?"

"I have to work late every Monday night," he says. "But I'm free on Sundays."

"The restaurant is closed on Sundays," I snap. "So let's just forget the whole idea. I don't think there's ever going to be a night when we all can get together."

"Hey, Dad, don't get upset. I really do want to go to dinner with you, but I've got a pretty busy schedule these days. You understand, don't you?"

He's right, of course. As kids get older, they have lives of their own to lead. They can't always find time to spend with me, no matter how much they might want to. I only hope they realize whose fault it will be if their father turns out to be a juvenile delinquent.

But the first kid who implies I never have time for him is gonna get his clock cleaned.

PREFACE: CHAPTER 11

# TABLE TALK

The comment that came from her 15-year-old at the dinner table was not something you would have heard on a typical episode of *Leave It To Beaver*. Wally never said words like those. He never had thoughts like those.

For a moment, the dining room was so quiet you could have heard a fork drop. Normally it is so loud at our dinner table you couldn't hear a fork*lift* drop.

In the uncomfortable silence that followed, the 15-year-old's mother looked at me.

"Could you imagine ever saying something like that in front of your parents?" she asked.

I agreed that I could not.

But that was then. And this — no matter how much some people wish it weren't — is now.

When I ate at my parents' table, there was no cable television. No Madonna. No Andrew Dice Clay.

When I ate at my parents' table, television was black and white, but never blue. It was an era of closed-mouth kisses and twin-bedded marriages. Record lyrics were not filled with sexual references although you could, I suppose, find a hint of prurience in "do-wap, do-wap," if you looked hard enough.

Movies came in two varieties: family entertainment or stag films your Uncle Charlie showed on the living-room wall to his poker buddies. The most whispered-about movie of my childhood was called *The Moon Is Blue*. My parents would not tell me exactly why I wasn't allowed to see it, but years later, I found out. The director, clearly one of the leading smut-mongers of his time, had allowed the words "virgin" and "mistress" to be included in the dialogue. Fortunately for him, Jesse Helms wasn't looking.

Somehow, though, we learned the words we weren't supposed to know, just as our fathers had learned the words they weren't supposed to know. Learned them and gloried in them and said them whenever possible to prove to our buddies, and to ourselves, that we were men of the world. The only time we pretended not to know them was in front of our parents.

By seventh grade, my vocabulary — not to mention my hormones — was out of control. On the day a particularly attractive substitute teacher appeared in our classroom, I slipped a note to my best buddy calling attention to some of her more attractive areas. My buddy scribbled an adolescent reply and sent it back to me. I smirked, slipped the note into my pants and forgot all about it.

Until two days later, when I came home from school and found my parents in the living room, grim-faced and tight-lipped. I knew immediately they had caught me at something. I just didn't know *which* something.

Doing the laundry that morning, I learned, my mother had gone through my pants pockets expecting, no doubt, to find snakes and snails and puppy dogs' tails. She found, instead, THE NOTE.

My parents demanded an explanation. I, naturally, denied all knowledge of the note, most of which was in my handwriting and all of which had been found in my pocket. The interrogation dragged on longer than a Supreme Court confirmation hearing. No final resolution was reached. They kept asking about the note. I kept lying about the note. Finally I was sent to my room, still protesting that I hadn't done it and promising never to do it again.

Looking back, I realize I was not a particularly perverted kid and my parents were not particularly prudish adults. But it was a time in which we never said things "like that" in front of our parents.

And that's the way our relationship remained. Whatever questions I might have had, whatever doubts I might have felt, whatever confusion I might have experienced, never were spoken in front of them. The right time for us to talk about things "like that" came and passed in embarrassed silence. In their eyes, I always was too young. I still was too young on the day they died.

But that was then and this is now. If our children do not share all their questions and doubts and confusions with us, at least they are able to mention subjects we never could have imagined talking about in front of our parents.

And if the price for that is an occasional comment that brings a moment of uncomfortable silence to the dinner table, well, I think most parents are old enough to hear them.

# CHAPTER 11

○○○○○○○○○○○

Some parents feel that one of the toughest parts of the job is cooking for their kids. Nothing could be further from the truth. Cooking for kids is easy if you remember one rule:

*Don't.*

I have prepared approximately 4,239,712 meals. My kids have appreciated approximately 0 of them. The nearest I ever came to a compliment was the day a 15-year-old looked up from his veal cordon bleu and declared, "This stuff is almost good enough to eat without catsup on it."

After a quarter of a century of that kind of praise, you'd think I'd give up, show them how to operate a can opener and tell them to simmer for themselves. But my career as a parent and stepparent has been one continual attempt to make life imitate advertising. The very next meal I carry to the table, I keep telling myself, is the one that will bring happy smiles to their lips and sparkles of delight to their eyes, just like in the television commercials.

One meal I carry to the table, for instance, is chicken *piccata* and angel hair pasta made with sun-dried tomatoes and a chiffonade of basil. It's the kind of menu you see every month in *Good Housekeeping*, with a headline that says, "Low-Cost Meals Guaranteed to Win High Praise From Your Family and Get You Elected to the Parents' Hall of Fame."

I spend half of Sunday morning shopping. I buy the most buxom chicken breasts. The greenest basil. The most expensive sun-dried tomatoes packed in the most virginal olive oil.

I spend most of Sunday afternoon cooking. I pound the chicken breasts into perfect fillets. I trim the basil into perfect strips. I cut the sun-dried tomatoes into perfect slices. I am a regular Julia Child without pantyhose.

By 5 p.m. the angel hair pasta is *al dente,* the chicken breasts are *piccata* and it is time to eat. I call my family to the table. When they are seated, I carry in the angel hair pasta with the sun-dried tomatoes and the chiffonade of basil.

"What's this stuff?" the 17-year-old demands, poking warily at his serving.

"Pasta," I reply. "You guys love pasta."

"Why is it so thin? Did you screw it up?"

"I didn't screw it up. It's called angel hair pasta," I explain.

Immediately the conversation turns to what part of the angel the hair has come from. The 15-year-old guesses "legs." The 12-year-old guesses "armpits." I stop the discussion before it gets to the 14-year-old.

"Who wants chicken?" I ask.

"It's flat," the 17-year-old declares, examining his fillet suspiciously.

Immediately the conversation turns to why the chicken breasts are so flat. The 15-year-old guesses "lack of exercise." The 12-year-old guesses "road kill." The 14-year-old opens his mouth.

"Don't say it," I warn.

"I was just gonna ask where the spaghetti sauce was," he says.

"You don't put sauce on this kind of pasta," I inform him.

"I can't eat it without sauce," he insists. He gets out of his chair and heads for the kitchen. A minute later he returns with a jug of store-bought spaghetti sauce. Immediately there is a wrestling match for the jug. When it ends, four servings of angel hair pasta and chicken *piccata* are floating in sauce that cost $1.87 a gallon.

They slurp their dinners. There are smiles on their lips, sparkles of delight in their eyes and spaghetti sauce stains on their shirts. It is just like in the television commercials.

Sort of.

Even though I have sacrificed an entire day preparing a meal that winds up looking like spaghetti-sauce soup, I am not really discouraged by their lack of appreciation. Any father who has been on duty for more than a month knows that sacrifice is a big part of the job. Fatherhood, in fact, is nothing more than a series of major sacrifices.

The dream of owning a Jaguar XKE becomes the reality of a station wagon with washable seats. A trip to Cancun is pre-empted be three trips to the orthodontist's. According to the by-laws in the Cub Scout handbook, father-son camp outs may only be scheduled on the same weekends you have tickets for the Super Bowl, the Masters or the seventh game of the World Series. Properly handled, though, major sacrifices eventually become their own reward.

"I hear that Mr. Leonard down the street is driving to the Masters in the Jaguar XKE he bought after he came back from Cancun," you are entitled to sigh after a major sacrifice. "You remember Mr. Leonard. He's the guy who didn't have four kids to send through college."

The minor sacrifices, on the other hand, are the ones that make you wonder if vasectomies can be made retroactive.

Shortly before noon on a beautiful Saturday, for example, I am in the kitchen. It is a glorious day, with blue skies, warm temperatures and not a kid in sight. All week I have looked forward to this moment and now I am going to savor it to the max. I am going to prepare a bean burrito for myself. Then I am going to carry it out to the patio, where I will eat it slowly, soak up the sun and pretend that I am in Cancun surrounded by bronzed senoritas.

I open a can of refried beans, spread it on a warm flour tortilla, top it with cheese and salsa and heat it in the microwave. As I am dropping a generous dollop of sour cream on top of my hot burrito, my 14-year-old wanders into the kitchen.

"What's that?" he asks.

"Bean burrito," I tell him.

"Looks great," he says. "I didn't have any breakfast."

"Maybe that's because you just got out of bed 15 seconds ago."

"Sleeping really makes me hungry," he persists. "Especially for Mexican food."

"Did you want me to make you a burrito?" I ask. When you have been in the fatherhood business as long as I have, you learn to understand even the subtlest kid.

"Well, okay, if it's not too much trouble."

I hand the kid my burrito and return to the counter to make another one for myself. As I am removing the plate from the microwave, her 15-year-old strolls into the kitchen.

"Cool," he says. "Burritos."

I start to explain that I have been waiting all week to eat this burrito. But I realize that since I have given one burrito to my 14-year-old, I can't refuse to give one to her 15-year-old. That's how stepfathers get bad p.r.

I hand him my burrito and return to the counter again. I scrape what remains of the refried beans from the can, spread them on the last flour tortilla and make my last-chance burrito. I am nearly to the patio door when her 12-year-old drifts into the kitchen. I am not sure how they do it. It must be some sort of Pavlovian reaction triggered by the sound of the microwave buzzer.

Before he has a chance to say a word, I hand him the burrito and return to the counter. There are no more refried beans. There are no more flour tortillas. There is not enough cheese to feed a dieting mouse. Not only does fatherhood mean I'm never going to get to Cancun, it means I can't even pretend to go.

Not that it matters. Even if I got to Cancun, my 17-year-old would show up and walk off with the last bronzed senorita.

What's worse, I'm not even going to get any mileage out of this sacrifice. How much guilt can you pile on a kid by looking at him 20 years from now and saying, "You ate my burrito"?

Feeding teen-age boys may be a thankless and endless task, but it is not necessarily like the stories you may have heard. Sure, it's true that teen-age boys eat a lot. Ask any parent of a teen-age boy and you will hear tales of bottomless pits, hollow legs and entire Thanksgiving turkeys being swallowed whole. Gather a group of teen-age boys' parents in the same room and inevitably the conversation will deteriorate into competitive complaining.

"My Bruce eats twice his weight in food every day," a mother will declare.

"So?" a father will counter. "My Jason eats four times his IQ."

"You call that eating?" another parent will scoff. "I took my Kyle to a McDonald's last week and they had to change the 'number served' sign 22 times before he got done ordering."

Not all of these claims are exaggerations. For the typical boy, adolescence is a perpetual feeding frenzy. There are, in fact, only three times a day when teen-age boys will not eat:

Breakfast, lunch and dinner.

I'm not sure what it is, but there's something about sitting down at a dining room table that wipes out a kid's appetite. It doesn't matter what you serve. The same kid who eats 14 hot dogs at a baseball game couldn't force down a cocktail wiener if you put it on his dinner plate.

One day I am preparing dinner for three when the 15-year-old crawls into the kitchen.

"Why are you crawling?" I inquire.

"I'm too weak from hunger to stand up," he moans. "When's dinner?"

"Two and a half minutes," I estimate. "There'll just be you and me and your mother eating tonight, so set the table for three."

"I don't think I have enough strength to lift a napkin," he groans. "Can I have something while I'm waiting?"

"No. You'll ruin your appetite for dinner."

"If I don't get something to eat right away, I won't last until dinner."

"Well, then, I guess that'll be one less plate for us to wash," I say. It's not that I'm unsympathetic to the plight of the hungry, but this is the same kid whose after-school snack consisted of last night's leftover pizza, tomorrow morning's breakfast doughnuts and next Sunday's standing rib roast. And our condo is not exactly littered with the skeletons of children who have starved to death while living with us.

Trying not to trip over the 15-year-old, who is lying in the middle of the kitchen floor, whimpering and licking the refrigerator door, I finish preparing dinner and carry it to the table.

"All right," I announce, "time to eat."

We sit down at the dining room table.

"Please pass the salad," my wife asks.

"Anybody want to split this baked bean with me?" the 15-year-old asks. "I can't eat the whole thing."

"I thought you were hungry," I say.

"I was. But I'm not now."

While his mother and I eat, the 15-year-old rolls his bean from one side of the plate to the other. When we have finished eating, the bean still is there. But it has 30,000 miles on it.

After dinner we get up and take our customary positions in the kitchen. My wife stands at the sink, rinsing. I stand at the dishwasher, loading. And the 15-year-old stands in front of the refrigerator. Looking for something to eat.

But when it comes to feeding kids, timing is not the only thing. Salesmanship is crucial, too. Especially with my 14-year-old.

We are cooking out one afternoon, for instance, and my 14-year-old is examining the contents of his hot dog bun.

"What kind of hot dog is this?" he asks his stepmother.

"Actually," she says, "it's really a . . . "

"Ballpark," I interrupt. "It's a ballpark hot dog."

"No," she says, "I think it's a . . . "

"Hot dog," I repeat, glaring at her behind the 14-year-old's back. "It's definitely a ballpark hot dog. Nolan Ryan cooked it personally on the pitcher's mound at the Astrodome."

Satisfied, the 14-year-old covers the meat, the bun and two thirds of his shirt sleeve with catsup. As he stuffs it all into his mouth, his stepmother pulls me aside.

"What was all that about?" she asks. "You know perfectly well that's not a hot dog. It's a bratwurst."

"I know that and you know that," I agree. "But if you tell this kid he's got a bratwurst in his mouth, that thing will come shooting out faster than a speeding bullet. We'll have bratwurst flying all over the yard."

"As long as he thinks it tastes good, what's the difference what it's called?" she asks. "I don't understand."

"Of course you don't. That's because you have two kids who will eat anything. Your 12-year-old will sample dishes straight out of gourmet magazines. Not only will your 15-year-old eat recipes that are printed in *Bon Appetit,* he'd eat the magazine."

"My kids *are* good eaters."

"Your kids would arm-wrestle the cat for his Nine Lives. My 14-year-old's not like them. He believes that three of the four basic food groups are inedible."

"I have noticed he's sort of a picky eater," she agrees.

"He'll only eat the orange Froot Loops."

"But that's not unusual. Most kids are fussy about a few things," she says.

"Fussy? This kid makes Morris the cat look like a glutton. He won't eat fish. He won't eat fruit. The only vegetables he'll eat are potato chips. The only meats he'll eat are hot dogs and chicken."

"That's not true. When we had leg of lamb last week, he ate the whole thing."

"Sure he did," I explain to her. "That's because I was able to convince him that it was a drumstick from a chicken that had been on steroids."

The 14-year-old finishes his bratwurst and returns for seconds.

"May I have another hot dog?" he asks.

"How about trying a bratwurst instead?" I suggest. "They're really very good."

"I hate bratwurst."

"Okay, then, have a hot dog."

I fork a bratwurst onto his bun.

"And while you're at it, try some of this on it," I say, pushing a cup of gazpacho toward him.

"What is it?" he asks.

"Chunky catsup," I reply.

"Cool," he says, pouring it onto his bratwurst.

When it comes to getting food into some kids, you can't spend too much time worrying about little things like truth in advertising.

If getting our kids to eat at home is next to impossible, taking them out to eat is one step from bankruptcy.

When my kids were little, taking them out to dinner was no big deal. I'd have a steak, my wife would have a chef's salad and we could fill up the kids with a package of saltine crackers and a few bites of food from our plates. The bill frequently ran in excess of $10, but it was worth it for an evening of family togetherness.

Times, kids and wives have changed, not to mention the price of family togetherness. As I discover when my wife suggests that we go out for dinner with our sons, three of whom have become teen-agers against our wishes.

We stuff the kids in the back seat of the car and drive to a restaurant that caters to families. Of which there are roughly four billion standing in line at the entrance when we arrive.

"There's an hour-and-a-half wait," the hostess tells us at the door.

"I'm not sure our kids can wait that long," I tell her. "They're pretty hungry."

"Sir, *everybody* in this line has kids who are hungry."

"Maybe it would help if I talked with the manager," I suggest.

"The manager's no longer here."

"He quit?"

"Some kids ate him."

I give the hostess our name and we work our way to the bar to wait for it to be called. Our kids order soft drinks. Every three minutes. After half an hour, they have so much caffeine in them they won't be able to sleep until next April and we have run up a bar bill big enough to choke Ed McMahon. As we are waiting for our 12th round of drinks, the 14-year-old discovers that the restaurant has video games in the back room. I hand them each a quarter and they slosh off to play. A minute later, they are back.

"We need more quarters," the 12-year-old announces. I hand them four more quarters. After that, they return every minute on the minute.

"I'm not a father, I'm a change machine," I complain to their mother after they make their ninth withdrawal. "Stick a dollar in my mouth and four quarters come out of my . . . "

"Relax," she interjects. ``As long as they're off playing video games, they're not standing here whining about how hungry they are." An instant later the 12-year-old is standing there whining about how hungry he is.

We order a plate of Buffalo wings for him from the bartender. The Buffalo wings arrive a few minutes later. Before the 12-year-old has time to drip more than half a dozen splotches of sauce on his new sweater, his brothers appear. We order three more plates of Buffalo wings. With soft drinks.

By the time my name is called, we have gone through six pounds of quarters, 12 gallons of soft drinks, four new sweaters and we are up to our thighs in chicken wing bones.

A waitress leads us to our table and passes out menus. The 17-year-old eats his.

A few minutes later the waitress returns to take our orders.

The 14-year-old, who gets fainting spells if I put a breaded fish stick on his plate at home, orders trout *amandine.*

The 15-year-old, who declared only this morning that he has decided to renounce his parents' ecologically and ethically irresponsible lifestyle, shave his head and become a vegetarian, orders a slab of barbecued ribs.

The 17-year-old, who announced only this afternoon that he has to lose eight pounds before midnight to "make weight" for wrestling, orders spaghetti. With a side of prime ribs.

The 12-year-old can't make up his mind.

"The hamburger sounds good because it comes with French fries," he says. "But lobster tails sound good, too. What comes with lobster tails?"

"A cut in your allowance," I inform him.

The waitress turns to me.

"Are you ready to order, sir?" she says.

"How are the saltines tonight?" I ask.

"Sir?" she replies, puzzled.

"Never mind," I tell her. "I'll just eat off the kids' plates."

Eating used food is not necessarily my first choice, but then, I'm used to it. Finishing the food on a kid's plate is one way you can distinguish a father from a normal man.

There are other indicators, of course.

Most fathers will have Sani-Flush stains on their forearms from reaching into toilets to rescue combs, contact lenses and entire families of Fisher-Price people. If they've been at it for any length of time, they'll have tattoos around their biceps that say "water line."

Fathers will have callouses on their index finger from flipping off lights that have been left on all over the house by kids who "must think we own large portfolios of electric company stock."

Fathers will have callouses on both eardrums from getting into the car, turning the key and discovering that the 16-year-old who drove it last had the radio cranked up loud enough to cause internal bleeding.

And, of course, they will have "plate cleaner's gut."

That's one of the major differences between mothers and fathers.

Mothers are the ones with harried looks on their faces, worry lines around their eyes and five pounds of empty gum wrappers in their purses. Mothers are the original litter baskets.

But fathers are the original garbage disposals.

They are the ones who intercept dinner dishes en route from the table to the trash can and polish off the remains because "there's enough food left on this plate to feed India." They are the final destination for leftovers that are not enough to save but are too much to throw away.

Fathers do not enjoy eating the food that other people have covered with catsup. But they develop an aversion to throwing away food the first time they notice that the bottom line on their grocery bill has hit triple digits.

There probably are mothers who are plate cleaners, too. But most of them lost their fear of throwing away food somewhere around the time they finished off the last two spoonfuls from the bottom of their 5,000th jar of strained apricots.

Fathers, on the other hand, frequently don't get into plate cleaning until later in life.

In our family, it's been my job ever since the dog died. The day after the wake, I notice a kid carrying a plate of food toward the garbage can.

"Where are you going with that?" I demand.

"I'm throwing it away," he replies.

"There's enough food on that plate to feed India," I point out. Originality is not a prerequisite for fatherhood.

"I'm full."

"Give it to me, I'll finish it. There's no sense throwing perfectly good food away."

I polish off half a porkchop, a small hill of mashed potatoes and a Mount Everest of green beans.

"How about you?" I ask his sister. "Are you going to eat that salad?"

"I'm stuffed."

"Pass it down here."

After a generation of passing it down here, a father's plate-cleaning instinct becomes automatic. One afternoon we wound up in a fast food place behind a bus full of junior high soccer players. When they left, it was obvious by what remained on their trays that their orders had been bigger than their stomachs.

If my wife hadn't stopped me, I would have gained 40 pounds.

But if a father doesn't eat the food that remains on the table after his kids have finished picking at it, eventually it becomes one of the ugliest words in a family's vocabulary:

*LEFTOVERS.*

At our house, we have a five-step procedure for dealing with leftovers.

**Step 1**: Carefully cover the leftovers with plastic wrap.

**Step 2**: Place the carefully wrapped leftovers in an air-tight plastic container.

**Step 3**: Put the air-tight plastic container into the refrigerator.

**Step 4**: Leave the leftovers in the refrigerator for a minimum of three weeks.

**Step 5**: Throw them away.

I'm not sure why we bother with the first four steps. It's probably a carryover from my childhood, when eating leftovers was our only defense against mothers who carped about all those hungry kids in other countries.

Stubbornly, I keep trying to ignore today's reality. And the reality is that a refrigerator today is nothing more than a halfway house between the microwave oven and the garbage can. It's just a place for leftovers to loiter until they get fuzzy.

With each succeeding generation, it seems, leftovers become less functional.

My grandmother could take a leftover green bean and turn it into 12 gallons of soup. My mother could take a pound of leftover pot roast and turn it into three small pot pies. Today we're lucky if six pounds of leftover ham winds up making a sandwich.

My family has included two wives, six kids, three cats, a dog and a guinea pig. As nearly as I can tell, I am the only one who has ever eaten a leftover. I'm doing my best, but it's a lonely battle. I'm still working on last Thanksgiving's cranberry sauce.

Every once in awhile I bring up the subject of leftovers with my wife. Like on the afternoon I walk into the kitchen while she is in the midst of sending a chicken breast to Step. 5.

"Why are you throwing away food that doesn't have fuzz on it yet?" I ask.

"Because nobody's going to eat it," she replies.

"My mother would have taken that chicken breast and turned it into a five-course dinner."

"Big deal," she counters. "My grandmother would have taken this leftover piece of rice and fed Shanghai with it. Kids are different now."

"Maybe we just need to be more imaginative in the way we handle them," I suggest.

"Fine," she says. "To go with this chicken breast we have leftover rigatoni and some leftover asparagus. Use your imagination and see what happens."

I search through my cookbooks. Incredibly enough, I find a recipe that calls for leftover chicken breast, rigatoni and asparagus. I combine the leftovers, sprinkle some Parmesan cheese on top and summon my family to dinner.

"What's this meat?" the 14-year-old asks. "It looks familiar."

"Impossible," I lie. "It's from a brand-new chicken. Not more than two hours ago she was running around in a barnyard trying to avoid an eager rooster."

"What a minute, I think I've seen this pasta somewhere before," says the 15-year-old.

"Yeah, I remember," agrees the 12-year-old. "We had it last week. That means this stuff is . . . "

*"LEFTOVERS,"* they shout in unison.

The cat still is wearing footprints from being caught in the stampede out of the dining room.

"Nice try," my wife says after the last pair of Nikes has disappeared.

"Just get the plastic wrap," I tell her.

# COMPROMISING POSITIONS

After a few years, the differences that had been drowned out by the sound of bells begin to make themselves heard.

Some of the differences are cosmetic.

When we met, I had a headful of unnaturally curly hair, which I had rewound every three months at a combination barber shop and drive-through hardware outlet. My hair was not really stylish, but it was convenient.

The curly hair barely survived the honeymoon.

"The Little Orphan Annie look is out," she said. "You need to go to a hair stylist."

So now I have naturally straight hair and a bathroom shelf filled with hair spray, gel, mousse and blow dryers. I spend 45 minutes messing with it every morning and it never looks the same two days in a row.

If my hair is not in the same shape it was when we met, neither is my wardrobe. Not one item of clothing survived the trip from my bachelor apartment to our marital condo. I used to have drawers full of T-shirts with the names of defunct taverns on the chests. Now I have drawers full sweaters in colors I never heard of, created by designers whose names I can't pronounce.

Some of the differences are caloric.

For most of my adult life, I looked forward to the day I could afford to splurge a bit at the grocery store; when I could move up to prime steaks and premium beer.

Two days after I got there, she began reading health books and determined that red meat is bad for my heart and beer is bad for my waistline.

Now I eat skinless chicken and grilled fish. Washed down with designer water. I don't like them, but she makes me eat them because they are good for me.

One of the biggest differences is cultural.

She comes from a hugging and kissing culture. Every time she and her family or friends get together, they hug and kiss. At large gatherings, by the time the last person has finished hugging and kissing "hello," the first person has started hugging and kissing "goodbye." I have missed entire meals waiting for a break in the hugging and kissing.

I grew up in a culture in which you didn't hug and kiss anyone you didn't plan to marry or take to a motel. With my friends, greetings are a non-contact activity, generally limited to conversations that go something like:

"Hey, how've you been?"

"Not bad."

"Fine. Where's the beer?"

Kissing becomes an issue with us on the day we are on our way home from her niece's wedding.

"Why don't you like my family and friends?" she demands as we are getting into the car.

"Who says I don't?"

"You never act like you do. You never kiss any of them."

"I never kiss any of the Cleveland Browns, either. That doesn't mean I don't like them. It's just the way I was raised."

"In my circle, everybody kisses."

"I've noticed. It's amazing that people in your circle have any lips left."

"Well, the least you could have done was be nicer to my niece," she says. "It *was* her wedding day."

"I thought I was very nice to her."

"It's traditional to kiss the bride, not punch her on the shoulder and muss up her hair."

"I didn't punch her. I tapped her. And it was a very sincere tap, at that."

"It was embarrassing," she replies.

"I'll try to do better," I promise. "The next time I meet one of your friends, I'll suck her face off."

Adjustment is what marriage is all about and we each have had to do our part. Her part has been as the adjustor. My part has been as the adjustee.

So now my hair is more stylish and my wardrobe is more fashionable. My insides are healthier and my outsides are trimmer. I kiss every member of her family, most of her friends and several of her enemies.

Considering how much adjusting I needed, it's hard to imagine exactly what she saw in me in the first place.

All I can figure is that she's the kind of woman who loves a challenge.

# CHAPTER 12

If adjustment is what puts a lock on wedded bliss, compromise is the key to that adjustment.

Compromise, in fact, is the essence of wedded bliss.

It is an art I failed to master in my first marriage. One of our biggest disagreements was about children. I wanted two. She wanted three. But I stuck to my guns and we did not have three. We had four.

This time, however, I have learned to compromise.

Take cooking out, which becomes a burning issue in the first summer of our marriage.

She likes cookouts. That probably comes from a lifetime of looking at magazine layouts in which models dressed in Ralph Lauren yuppie clothes pose on terraces with swimming pools and BMWs in the background, eating things like grilled prawns stuffed with mesquite-smoked raddichio and pretending to enjoy themselves.

I, on the other hand, see the whole cookout thing for what it is: a sexist scam invented in the mid-50s by women who would do anything to get out of the kitchen in the summer, even if it meant eating hamburgers that looked like hockey pucks, but weren't as tender. Somehow they have managed to con husbands into believing it's macho to put on an apron with a dopey saying on the front and stand on the patio in the hot sun chewing smoke while the rest of the family sits inside in the air-conditioning and eats all the appetizers.

But not me. As I told her on the day we met, "Hi. I'm a Virgo, I've had a vasectomy and I don't do cookouts."

So we reached a compromise. It was item No. 1 in the prenuptial agreement. It was, in fact, the *only* item in the prenuptial agreement. Since she already owned a gas grill, I would agree to having occasional cookouts on our patio. But if she insisted on eating burnt food, she would have to burn it herself.

As Donald Trump found out, a prenuptial agreement is not always worth the disappearing ink it is written with. On a Sunday afternoon of our first summer together, I find myself on the patio, chewing smoke.

But it is a compromise.

She has invited her Aunt Ruth and Uncle Walt for dinner. Fine people, Aunt Ruth and Uncle Walt. Just the kind of folks you want to have around when you're in the mood for a minute-by-minute reminiscence of the Great Depression.

"I thought maybe you'd like to cook out for them," my wife says. "I have some drumsticks in the refrigerator marinating in salad oil."

"Well, I hope you're in the mood for chicken tartare, because I'm not going to stand out there and cook," I inform her.

"Fine," she says. "I'll do the cooking and you can sit inside and entertain my Aunt Ruth and Uncle Walt."

Aunt Ruth and Uncle Walt arrive at 2 p.m. At 2:05 I put on an apron with a dopey saying on it and head for the patio with 10 pounds of well-oiled chicken legs, two pounds of which slither off the tray as I am closing the patio door. I pick up the legs, wipe them on the apron with the dopey saying and toss them onto the pre-heated gas grill.

Three seconds later a burst of flame big enough to impress Mrs. O'Leary's cow erupts and engulfs the chicken legs. As I am beating out the fire with a long-handled spatula, it occurs to me that I may have pre-heated the grill a degree or two too high. After the last flame has been rendered unconscious, I turn down the controls.

I stand in front of the grill and wait for the chicken to cook. Through the patio door I can see my family in the living room. They are laughing. Why shouldn't they be? They're not the ones standing out here with the sun in their eyes and the smoke following them wherever they go.

After several minutes, it is time to immolate the other side of the chicken. I grasp the end of a drumstick with long-handled tongs and turn it. The bone turns easily. The meat, on the other hand, stays exactly where it was — fused to the grill.

I drop the bone onto the tray and try another leg. I wind up with another bone. In no time at all I have two pounds of bones on the tray and eight pounds of chicken stuck to the grill.

As I am chipping dinner off the grill with a long-handled jack hammer, the 12-year-old walks out onto the patio. He looks at the tray.

"What's with all the bones?" he wants to know.

"I'm going to archaeology school and that's my homework assignment," I snap.

The 12-year-old stares at me. It is obvious he doesn't understand. If he's lucky, he never will. If he's lucky, he'll marry a vegetarian and they will live in a land where there is no summer.

After we have fed Aunt Ruth and Uncle Walt ("I haven't had chicken bones like that since the Great Depression, my boy"), we kiss them goodbye and walk back to the patio to debrief the disaster.

"I don't think it was your fault," my wife allows. "It's this old grill. The grate is all rusted and the coals are corroded. We need to buy a new one. And, while we're at it, we need new patio furniture."

At this point, I realize, it is time to calmly and maturely discuss the issue and then reach a compromise.

I begin the discussion.

"We're not spending all that money on a stupid grill and stupid stuff for the stupid patio," I shout, calmly.

"It's not stupid stuff," she yells back, maturely.

"Yes it is."

"No it isn't."

"Is too."

"Is not."

Eventually, of course, we are able to reach a compromise. We buy a new grill the next day. But we do not get the new patio furniture until the following week. Compromising is easy, once you get the hang of it.

I'd probably be more enthusiastic about the new grill and the new patio furniture if it didn't take up so much space in the backyard. Not that her backyard is the only reason I married her, of course. Even if she didn't have just the right amount of tillable soil surrounding the patio in the back of her condo, I would have proposed to her. Most likely.

But the backyard doesn't hurt. Especially when we get to the planting season.

One of the disadvantages of living in a bachelor apartment was that there was no place to grow things. Unless you count whatever it was that sprouted in the 20-year-old's clothes hamper while he was away at college.

Her condo, on the other hand, includes just enough land for a small garden. So when I wake up one morning and discover that spring seems to have arrived, I jump out of bed and start to work. By the time she comes downstairs, I have nearly finished.

"What's that diagram?" she asks when she sees me working at the kitchen table.

"I've mapped out what we'll be able to plant this year," I explain. "See, along the fence we can put in half a dozen tomato plants. The green beans can go here in the back, next to the strawberry patch. And I figure this area around the air conditioner will be perfect for zucchini. How does that sound?"

"Not bad," she says. "And where are you planning to put the soy beans and alfalfa?"

"Why would we plant soy beans and alfalfa?"

"We're going to need something to feed the livestock with, aren't we?"

"What are you trying to tell me?"

"I'm trying to tell you that I don't want to have the only condo in this complex that qualifies for agricultural price supports. In case you hadn't noticed, when our neighbors come home from work most of them are driving Toyotas or BMWs, not John Deeres."

"Planting a few vegetables won't exactly turn this place into Green Acres," I point out. "Besides, it doesn't make sense to let the ground go to waste out there."

"It's not going to go to waste. I've already made plans for the garden. I'm going to be planting *anemone, dianthus, clematis* and *ranunculus*."

"That sounds like the starting backfield for the Vatican football team," I note. "But I suppose I probably can find recipes for them in one of my cookbooks. What kind of dishes do you make with them?"

"You don't make any kind of dishes with them."

"You mean you can't eat them?"

"Of course not. They're flowers."

"If you can't eat them, what good are they? What's the point of getting dirt under your fingernails planting something you can't saute with garlic and onions?"

"They'll beautify our lives."

"Ten or fifteen bucks a week less for produce on our grocery bill would beautify our lives," I point out.

"You can't put a price tag on aesthetics."

"Maybe not. But you can put a price tag on what this mob of ours eats for dinner. If we grow a few bushels of tomatoes, at least I can make spaghetti sauce out of them. That makes more sense than planting a lot of silly flowers with names that would stop a spelling bee. But, I'll tell you what. Let's compromise. I'll plant tomatoes along the fence and you can plant your flowers on the other side of the patio around the air conditioner. In fact, I've already cleared all the weeds out of that area for you."

"What weeds?"

"The weeds around the air conditioner."

"Those weren't weeds. Those were the *columbine* I planted two years ago. What else did you murder? My rose bush? My tulips? My magnolia tree?"

Apparently there is not enough room in our backyard for compromise. And there's not a whole lot of it on the inside of the condo, either. Especially when it comes to control of the air conditioning.

I'll be the first to admit that two marriages and a blind date do not necessarily make me an expert on the subject of female physiognomy. But even my limited research leads me to believe that men and women do not hear the same message when they call time and temperature.

My first mate and I were married for 22 years, 17 of which she spent standing in the hallway turning up the thermostat.

My second mate, on the other hand, apparently believes that you can never be too thin, too rich or too cool. The details are hazy, but I'm pretty sure that the document I signed on our wedding day was a marriage certificate. She seems to think it was a consent form giving her permission to have my body frozen in our living room. While I am still alive.

She starts practicing cryogenics without a license on the first day of summer. Which, according to her, is the day after the last measurable snowfall. By the beginning of June, she has the dial set on "frostbite." By the Fourth of July it's down to "hypothermia." To our neighbors, we become known as the couple that lives in the house of blue lips.

On the first warm morning of our marriage I wake up and discover that my nose hairs are frozen together. Grabbing a blanket and wrapping it around my shoulders, I shuffle out of the bedroom. I am halfway down the stairs when she looks up. Probably because she has heard my teeth chattering.

"Why are you walking so slowly?" she asks.

"I don't want to slip on the ice."

"What ice?"

"Any place this cold has got to have ice. Maybe we'd better throw some rock salt on these steps."

"Don't tell me you think it's cold in here?"

"I don't think it's that bad. But there's a penguin in our closet trying to find an electric blanket."

"If it were any warmer in this place we could grow orchids in the dining room," she says.

"There's frostbite on my sunburn," I point out.

"A cactus plant in the kitchen keeled over this morning from heat prostration," she counters, as the air conditioning kicks on again and sends a blast of arctic air up my shorts.

"We have the only condo on the block with a wind chill factor," I parry.

"You can't be cold," she says. "There are beads of sweat on your forehead."

"They're not beads of sweat. They're icicles," I chatter. "This isn't a condo, it's a three-bedroom igloo."

It doesn't take a certified meteorologist to forecast that the rest of the summer will be a three-month battle for control of the thermostat. Nearly every morning I get out of bed, shiver my way downstairs and turn off the air conditioner. Except for those mornings when I can't get out of bed because my head is frozen to the pillow.

I'd like to compromise on this issue, but we seem to have irreconcilable differences when it comes to the definition of a comfortable temperature. My feeling is that the temperature is not comfortable if the warmest place in a house is the refrigerator's crisper drawer.

Even if I could get her to turn off the air conditioning, it still would be cold in our kitchen, though. The kitchen always has been the coolest room in the place. It's been that way in every house I've ever lived. It didn't matter if you pushed the thermostat to triple figures. You still would be able to see your breath in the kitchen.

I used to wonder why, until I came across an item in the paper that said researchers have determined that the average person opens the refrigerator door 22 times a day.

Suddenly it all makes sense.

I am an average person, which means that I open the refrigerator door 22 times a day and a little bit of cold leaks out each time. That makes the temperature in the kitchen drop a degree.

My wife is an average person, which means that she opens the refrigerator door 22 times a day and a little bit more cold leaks out each time. That makes the temperature drop another degree.

And our sons are average teen-age persons. That explains the frost on the outside of the microwave.

As average teen-age persons, they make so many visits to the refrigerator the biceps on their door-opening arms are two inches larger than on their other arms and they have permanent frostbite on the tops of their heads.

I'm not sure why they bother. Like all teen-age persons, they already know "there's nothing to eat in there." But apparently some morbid curiosity keeps bringing them back.

One Saturday morning I sit down at the kitchen table with a piece of paper and a pencil to keep track of their pilgrimages to the refrigerator.

Shortly after the crack of noon the first teen-ager of the day lurches into the kitchen, wearing boxer shorts and bed hair. He goes directly to the refrigerator, pulls open the door and shoves his bed hair inside. Ten or 15 minutes later he emerges, empty-handed.

"Not hungry?" I inquire.

"There's nothing in there to eat," he replies. "There's *never* anything in there to eat."

"You're right," I agree. "The only reason we even bought that refrigerator is so we'd have some place to hang Ann Landers columns."

He searches through the pantry, which also is stuffed with nothing to eat. Thirty seconds later he returns to the refrigerator and opens the door again. Obviously he is under the impression that while the door is closed someone sneaks through the back of the refrigerator and stocks it with new items.

Again he is unable to find any food worth putting into his mouth.

"Why don't you have some scrambled eggs?" I suggest.

"It's too early for eggs," he says. "Do we have any pizza left over from last night?"

"I don't know," I admit. "Have you looked under your brothers' beds?"

He returns to the refrigerator.

"I'm really hungry," he moans.

"I'm not surprised. You can work up a pretty good appetite from all the exercise you're getting opening that refrigerator door."

By my count, in the next half hour he opens the refrigerator door exactly 31 times, shuts it exactly 18 times and takes out exactly no food. After that I stop keeping track. My fingers have become too numb to hold the pencil.

No matter what the temperature, marriage is just one great compromise after another.

Of course, reaching compromises means that you actually have to listen to each other. Listening, most authorities agree, is crucial to a marriage. Seventy-three percent of all failed marriges began to crumble the first time she insisted, "We have to have a serious talk," and he responded, "No problem, it's almost halftime."

But it is not enough merely to listen to the words of your mate. You must also understand what they mean. The process is called "interpretive listening."

When I say, for instance, that I am going to stop with my Wednesday night tennis league buddies for "a quick one," she knows there is no sense keeping dinner warm. If I say I am going to stop with my Wednesday night tennis league buddies for "a few," she does not expect to see me again until Friday.

I am not nearly as fast a learner as she is. But I am starting to hear between her lines. On a Friday evening when we are dressing to go out for a party, this is what she says *(and this is what I hear)*:

"I'll be ready on time."

*(She'll be ready today.)*

"We won't be late."

*(We'll get there before the last guest has gone home.)*

"I'll be ready soon."

*(She is standing in her bathrobe in front of a closet roughly the size of Bloomingdale's women's department muttering to herself, "I don't have a thing to wear.")*

"I'm hurrying as fast as I can."

*(She's on the phone, calling around to see if any of her friends has a black wool skirt she can borrow.)*

"It's not going to do you any good to keep bugging me."

*(It's not going to do me any good to keep bugging her.)*

"I'm working on it."

*(She has undone the top button on her bathrobe.)*

"I'm getting there."

*(She has decided what to wear and she is trying it on.)*

"Yuk."

*(She has changed her mind.)*

"I don't have a single pair of shoes."

*(She doesn't have as many shoes as Imelda Marcos.)*

"Have you seen my taupe satin pumps?"

*(She knows full well that I wouldn't know the difference between a taupe satin pump and a sump pump. And that the odds of me finding them are roughly the same as my chances of finding the Loch Ness monster. It is possible that she does not even own a pair of taupe satin pumps. But looking for them will give me something to do while I'm waiting.)*

"It won't be long now."

*(She has started polishing her nails.)*

"I'm practically ready."

*(She has found a pair of pantyhose without a runner in them.)*

"I'm all dressed."

*(She has her blouse on.)*

"I'm almost ready."

*(She has her skirt on.)*

"Two more minutes."

*(I have time to send out for pizza.)*

"I just have to put on my makeup."

*(I have time to fly to Naples and pick up a pizza.)*

"I'm all ready."

*(It's time for me to start getting dressed.)*

Learning to listen is only one side of the marital coin. The flip side is learning to shut up. Because when I point out that we did not actually wind up walking out the front door until three hours after she said she was ready, what I hear next is:

"That's because I have nothing to wear."

One of the many mysteries of married life is how nothing to wear can fill an 11-foot by 4-foot walk-in closet. But some mysteries are best left uninvestigated and at this point I have one of two options. I can murmur something sympathetic and walk away. Or I can open my big fat mouth and shove my Reebok into it.

"Nothing to wear?" my big fat mouth exclaims before I can plug it with a shoe. "How can you say that? Diana Ross doesn't have as many clothes as you do. Madonna would love to . . . "

"That shows how much you know," she interrupts. "It just looks like I have a lot of clothes because all the hangers are full."

"Let me see if I have this straight. All those things on hangers *aren't* clothes?"

"Of course they're clothes," she says, impatiently. "But they're all old and out of style."

"Well, then, why don't you get rid of them and buy some new ones?"

The look on her face tells me that I am listening, but I am not really hearing.

"You don't seriously expect me to throw away clothes," she demands.

"Sure. Why not?"

"Which clothes, exactly, would you like me to get rid of?"

"How about that wedding dress?"

"You want me to throw away the dress from our wedding?"

"It's not from *our* wedding. It's from your first marriage."

"I don't care. You don't throw away a wedding dress. You save it in case one of your children wants to wear it on their wedding day."

"So which one of our sons do you think is going to want to walk down the aisle in it?"

"Throwing away the wedding dress isn't the answer," she says. "There's only one logical solution. Instead of me throwing away any clothes, let's compromise and make more room for them in the closet."

"How are we going to do that? As it is, all my clothes are on one hanger. Unless you just want me to hang my stuff on a doorknob."

"You don't have to move your clothes. We just have to expand the closet space."

"Good idea," I agree. "We can knock out that wall at the end of the closet and expand it into the bathroom, which I only get to use once a week anyway, so it would be no real problem to move your sweaters whenever I have to . . . "

"What I meant was, I want to call one of those companies that come and reorganize your closets to give you more space."

The next day a man from a closet reorganizing company arrives at our house to look into our clothing. He stands as close to the closet as he can get without being buried in blouses and studies it for several seconds.

"It's pretty crowded in there," he says to me. "Which hanger is yours?"

"Third from the end," I reply.

"You're lucky," he says. "A lot of husbands just get the doorknob."

He takes some measurements, draws some sketches to show how the closet would be rearranged and hands us a cost estimate. The number on the bottom line is $657.45.

For that amount, someone will come out and install some shelves and some rods. Which will give us more space in our closet. Which will allow my wife to buy more clothes. Which means we will be able to go out more often for expensive evenings. It is, my wife assures me, a terrific bargain.

But it's a mystery to me.

Unfortunately, she is not the only member of my family with whom I have to reach compromises.

It is shortly before dawn one morning, for instance, and I am doing what I do best: sleeping my brains out.

It is a satisfying sleep, made even more enjoyable by a dream which, as nearly as I can recall, has something to do with Marla Maples and a long feather. The details are hazy, but I remember her saying something about being sick of yachts and diamonds and what she really wanted all along was a middle-aged newspaper writer who could take her bowling. She is purring and calling me "The D.L." And then she produces this long feather and starts to brush it gently across my forehead, then down my cheek and over my lips and . . .

Which is when I wake up and realize that it is not a dream. Something really is brushing across my face. I open one eye. The first thing I see is not Marla. It is not even Ivana.

It is the southern end of a northbound cat.

"Get out of my face," I mumble.

My stepcat gets out of my face and gets *on* my face. Gently, but firmly, he walks across my forehead, then down my cheek and over my lips. He does not stop walking until he has left footprints on 90 percent of my body. Worn out by his journey, he curls up between my legs. I spit the fur out of my mouth and drift back to sleep.

Since I became the stepfather of a cat, the only nights his mother and I have slept alone were on our honeymoon in Portugal. And that was only because the cat's passport had expired.

I resisted at first. On the first night after our honeymoon I close the bedroom door, turn on Johnny Carson and crawl into bed.

"What are you doing?" my bride asks.

"Television helps me get to sleep," I explain. "Baseball games really are the best, but at this time of night they don't . . . "

"I meant, why did you close the bedroom door?"

"Why shouldn't I? Were you expecting company?"

"No. But the cat is going to be very unhappy," she says. "He's used to sleeping with me."

"He'll just have to get over it," I declare. "I'm not sharing my bed with anyone who has chipmunk breath."

I roll over and go to sleep. Thirty winks later I am awakened by a thumping on the bedroom door.

"I don't know which kid that is," I shout. "But if you don't quit pounding on our door, that hand will never be able to hold another joystick."

The thumping continues. Annoyed, I throw off the covers, get out of bed and yank open the door. A bag of fur with bruised knuckles dashes into the room. By the time I get back to bed, the bag of fur is lying on my pillow. Smirking.

"You're on my pillow," I point out. I suppose I can find room in our bed for him, but I refuse to let him have my pillow.

My new stepcat looks up at me, blinks twice, lifts one hind leg until it is behind his ear and begins to clean himself.

"All right, keep the pillow," I concede, wedging my way into the bed.

"But I want at least a third of the blanket."

It's been that way ever since. My wife gets half the bed. My stepcat gets my pillow. And I get to hang over the edge of the mattress, clinging to the box spring to keep from falling out.

It's not such a bad compromise, really. But I sure hated telling Marla she had to sleep on the couch.

Preface: Chapter 13

# Holidays

A *menorah* will glow in our house this December. For eight consecutive evenings, one additional candle will be lighted to commemorate the eight days of *Hanukkah*, the Jewish Feast of Lights.

In the same month, the glow in our living room will be from a Christmas tree. There will be a star on top of the tree to represent the one that guided wise men to Bethlehem.

Some people are uncomfortable with the thought of a *menorah* and a Christmas tree being lighted in the same house.

There are Jews who worry about assimilation, which many consider a greater threat to their existence than the Holocaust. They feel that children will not grow up true to their faith if they are raised in a home where one parent is not Jewish.

There are Christians who would prefer a society in which everyone believes as they do. They feel that children should be taught that there is one true religion. One exclusive path to Heaven.

Both of those things may be so.

But, in our house, there is room for the glow of more than one light in a month that is supposed to be dedicated to peace on earth, good will to men.

On at least one night in December, our sons will stand together and watch the flame pass from the *shammash* candle to the other candles. They will hear words recited that they will not understand. They will play with a four-sided top called a *dreidel.*

I have no reason to believe that watching a candle being lighted and hearing words that they do not understand and eating potato pancakes with apple sauce or sour cream will cause my sons to desert the religion in which they grew up.

But it may affect them in other ways.

It may let them understand, in a way that no words can, that there are other beliefs.

Other religions.

Other lights.

On Christmas morning our sons will sit together in front of a Christmas tree and watch the reflection of lights in the ornaments and the icicles. They will hear carols that are vaguely familiar to them. They will eat candy canes and drink eggnog. They will rip open mountains of presents.

I don't think any of these things will sway her son's faith in the religion of his father. He has grown up with the message of Christmas all around him.

So the light of a *menorah* and the light of a Christmas tree will glow in our house again this year. And maybe some people will be uncomfortable with that. But I'm pretty sure that somewhere I read:

*"And the Lord said, 'let there be light.' And there was light. And it was good."*

I don't remember it saying that the light was better if it came from a *menorah* or if it came from a Christmas tree.

# CHAPTER 13

○○○○○ ○○○○○○○○

**B**ecause of the differences in our religious and cultural backgrounds, the early months of our marriage are filled with a great deal of learning.

I learn about such holidays as *Hanukkah* , Passover and *Yom Kippur.* I learn not to ask for tartar sauce with my *gefilte* fish. I learn how to pronounce *challah* at a *seder* dinner without generating a roomful of hysterical laughter.

When we get to our first Christmas together, it is her turn. It will be our first Christmas tree. Just as lighting the *menorah* on *Hanukkah* is a part of her culture, decorating a Christmas tree is a part of mine. And it is one of my favorite traditions. Picking the tree. Bringing the decorations out of the attic. Untangling the lights. Stringing the lights. Hanging fragile glass ornaments next to a child's handmade decoration made of a toilet paper roll and gift wrap.

As Christmas approaches, I mention the subject.

"How do you feel about having a Christmas tree in the house?" I ask her.

"I don't see any problem," she says. "After all, this is your house, too. Besides, I think a Christmas tree would look lovely in front of the living room window. You'd be able to see the velvet bows from outside."

"What velvet bows?"

"The velvet bows we're going to tie on the Christmas tree. Just because I've never decorated a Christmas tree doesn't mean I don't know what they're supposed to look like. I've seen plenty of pictures in my decorating magazines."

"Those aren't real Christmas trees," I explain. "A real Christmas tree has all sorts of different ornaments on it. They don't have to match, or anything. In fact, the more cluttered it is, the better. It's sort of like getting a pizza with everything."

"Just what I've always wanted. A tree in my living room with pepperoni, mushrooms and anchovies hanging from it."

"You're missing the point. Putting up a Christmas tree isn't something you hire an interior decorator to do. It's something the whole family takes part in. Everybody gets to hang the ornaments they like. That way, the tree becomes an expression of everyone's individual taste."

"So, what are you going to be hanging, beer cans?"

"Don't be silly. Beer cans look terrible on a Christmas tree." At least they did on the last tree I had in my bachelor apartment.

"All right," she says, "let me see if I have this straight. We're going to bring a tree in here and decorate it by mob rule, with no cohesion, no sense of style, no attention to . . . "

"It's a Christmas tree," I interrupt, "not an *objet d'art*. Anyway, once you cover it with icicles it will look fine."

"Icicles? You don't mean those tacky aluminum things that cling to people's clothes when they walk by and wind up hiding in the living room carpet until the following August?"

"You've got to have them," I say. "They cover up the bare spots."

"Instead of covering up the bare spots, why don't we just buy a perfect tree in the first place?" she asks.

"There is no such thing as a perfect Christmas tree."

"That's not true. I drove past a lot yesterday where they were selling them and practically every tree was perfect."

"Of course they were. That's because they were still on the lot. They don't develop bare spots until you tie them to the top of your car. While you're driving home, they start pulling off their own limbs. Finding the right corner in the living room to hide the worst side of the tree can be a real headache."

"This whole subject is giving me a real headache," she says. "If we're going to have a Christmas tree, let's do it right. We'll have one delivered by Sak's and I'll make some pretty velvet bows, probably in mauve, to tie to the. . . "

It is not exactly the Christmas tree I had in mind, but then, our marriage is a continuing learning experience. I can't wait until spring, when she teaches me how to dye Easter eggs.

Not only do I have to introduce her to the subtleties of Christmas tree decorating, I have to give her a quick lesson in the realities of my family's style of Christmas shopping. It is a crash course that takes place as we are in the final frenzy of holiday hysteria.

We have elbowed our way through 17 department stores. We have run out of gas three times while circling a shopping mall in search of an empty parking spot. We have witnessed a fistfight between two shoppers arguing over a $19.95 cotton tablecloth embroidered with the words, "Peace on Earth, Good Will to Men."

And, as we are standing in a checkout line where a seasonal employee has spent the last half hour trying to figure out how to open the cash register drawer, the stepmother of my children turns to me and asks:

"Aren't we done shopping yet?"

"Not quite," I tell her. "We still need one more present for my 15-year-old."

"What else are you planning to get for him?"

"It really doesn't matter," I admit. "Just as long as it costs $23.82."

"I don't understand."

"I'm not sure I understand it myself. All I know is, if I don't spend exactly the same amount of money on each of my kids' presents, you'll need a magnifying glass to find holiday cheer in our living room on Christmas morning."

"I'm sure you're exaggerating," she says.

"Maybe," I concede. "But we're talking about my kids, the ones who used to sit at the breakfast table every morning counting the Cheerios in their bowls to make sure nobody else got more than they did."

"Sounds like some pretty intense sibling rivalry," she agrees. "But certainly they're not going to be that way on Christmas morning. Christmas is such a peaceful holiday."

"Are you kidding? Christmas morning is the sibling rivalry World Series. If you buy one kid a 10-speed bike and another kid a 400-piece Lincoln Log set, the kid who got the bike will insist he still has another 399 presents coming to him."

"Let me see if I've got this straight," she says. "If you buy three $30 shirts for one kid and a pair of $90 basketball shoes for a second kid, the one who got the shoes will complain because he only got one present?"

"You're on the right track, but I'm afraid you still haven't grasped all the nuances," I point out. "The kid who got the three shirts will complain because his brother got four presents."

"'Four?"

"Two shoes and two shoelaces."

"And this happens every Christmas?" she asks.

"Invariably," I sigh. "We even had problems the year we bought them all the same number of presents and spent exactly the same amount of money on each one."

"How could that have been a problem?"

"One kid pouted until Groundhog Day because his presents weighed less than his brothers' presents."

By the time I have finished explaining the Christmas facts of life to her, we are next in line at the register. In desperation, I grab a sweater off the counter for the 15-year-old.

"How much for this?" I ask the sales clerk, who is trying to open the cash register drawer with her nail file.

"It comes to $21.20 with tax," she says.

"No you don't," I say, whipping out my checkbook. "I'm paying $23.82 for this sweater and not a penny less."

"Did you want to have it gift-wrapped?" the clerk asks.

"Better let me see what it weighs first," I tell her.

But for a woman whose cultural roots never grew in the yule garden, my wife has some pretty definite opinions about Christmas gift giving. And it is no real surprise that her list looks nothing like mine.

My list includes immediate relatives, close friends and anyone important enough to be included in my will. Or anyone whom I suspect might include me in *their* will.

Her list is a bit longer.

It includes immediate relatives, intermediate relatives and distant relatives. Close friends, casual acquaintances and nicely dressed strangers. Neighbors, the immediate relatives of neighbors, close friends of the immediate relatives of neighbors and any person she has ever met at a party, a PTA meeting or a garage sale. If you went more than three floors on an elevator with her at any time during the past year, you're probably on her Christmas gift list.

She is the type of person a Beverly Hills psychologist must have been writing about in a newspaper story dealing with taking the stress out of Christmas.

"Remember," the psychologist advised in the article, "you are under no obligation to spend money you don't have on people you don't care about."

I am tempted to show the article to my wife, but I decide against it. Not only wouldn't it do any good, she'd probably buy *him* a present, too.

But the psychologist's message is pretty much the same as the one I try to deliver when we find ourselves in the shopping mall parking lot and discover that the Christmas presents she has bought won't fit into the car.

"Maybe we need a station wagon," she suggests.

"Maybe we need a sleigh with eight tiny reindeer," I counter. "Exactly who are all these gifts for, anyway?"

"Just the people on my list," she says, hauling a piece of paper out of her purse. Not only are they not people I care about, they are people I've never heard of. It's not a Christmas list, it's a telephone directory.

"Who *are* these people?" I demand.

"Well, some of them are people I work with. Then, of course, there's my hair stylist, my manicurist, the mailman, the paperboy, the UPS deliveryman, my gynecologist, my dentist, the kids' pediatrician, the cat's veterinarian, the lady who had the Tupperware party . . ."

"I hope you didn't forget the cab driver who took us to the airport last

August," I interrupt.

"What are you trying to say?"

"I'm trying to say that your Christmas shopping is getting out of hand. Do we really have to buy presents for all these people?"

"Don't you want to thank the people who have made your life a little more pleasant during the past year?" she asks.

"I've already taken care of the bartender at the Pub. Besides, if making my life more pleasant was the criteria I used for deciding who should get Christmas presents, there are a couple of kids at home who might have trouble making the list."

"You can do whatever you want, Ebenezer," she replies. "But I happen to believe that giving presents at Christmas is what makes the season so special."

Yes, Virginia, there *is* a Santa Claus.

And I married her.

Whatever their backgrounds, there are differences between husbands and wives that transcend culture. I read a poll once about household chores. According to the survey, wives do 76 percent of the laundry, 73 percent of the cooking and 64 percent of the toilet bowls.

In defense of husbands, all I can say is:

"Yeah. But who does the Christmas lights?"

I took a poll of my own proving that, in our condo development, 100 percent of the husbands put up the Christmas lights while 100 percent of the wives came outside after the job was done and said, "You've got an orange one next to a red one."

I'm not sure who decided that perching on a wobbly stepladder and hanging by your teeth from the rain gutter was a husband's job. All I know is, on the first Saturday in December when the wind-chill factor is lower than my IQ, my wife walks into the living room, sees me sitting in a warm chair in front of the television and says, "Do you realize you're the only husband in our complex sitting inside watching a football game today?"

"So?" I reply. Or something equally witty.

"That's because all those other guys are out hanging Christmas lights so their condos will reflect the beauty of the season, bringing to their families the joy of . . . "

Sighing, I get out of my warm chair and look for the Christmas lights before she can break into a chorus of "Up on the rooftop, click, click, click."

I find the outdoor Christmas lights in a closet, where they have spent the last 11 months tying themselves into knots. I spend two hours unknotting them. I carry them outside, put them on the front porch and go to the storage shed. I spend another hour trying to separate the stepladder from the garden hose. I carry the stepladder to the front of the condo.

While I was arguing with the stepladder in the storage shed, I discover, the Christmas lights have tied themselves into knots again.

As I am untying the Christmas lights for the second time, I keep a wary eye on the stepladder. If I don't watch it every second, I know it will run back to the storage shed and re-tangle itself in the garden hose. Inanimate objects do not like me.

By the time I am actually ready to hang the lights, the temperature has dropped to 12 degrees below frostbite. I stand in front of the condo with a brisk wind whistling in one ear and out the other. I size up the situation.

The first thing I notice about the situation is that we own a two-story condo and a one-story stepladder. The lights would look beautiful stretched across the top of the condo, but the only way to get to the top of the condo would be to climb out a second floor window, throw a rope around the chimney and shimmy up to the roof. Unless I want to rent a helicopter.

I decide that the lights would look just as beautiful stretched across the top of the porch.

I open the stepladder, put the back two legs in the grass, the front two legs in the flower garden and start climbing to the top of the porch. As I climb, I can't help but notice that I do not seem to be getting any higher. The reason, I learn, is because the front legs of the stepladder are sinking into the flower garden. Eventually, it is sinking faster than I can climb. By the time I get to the top of the ladder, I'm pretty sure I will be lower than I was when I started.

I decide that the lights would look every bit as beautiful wrapped around the two pine trees that flank the porch. I stand back, lob a string of lights to the top of each tree, plug them in and head for the warmth of the living room.

Before I can get to my chair, my wife comes outside, stands in front of the condo, looks at the lights and says, "You've got an orange one next to a red one."

Hey, do I tell her how to clean the toilet bowl?

Partly because it does not come encumbered with the complications of conflicting religions — or tangled strings of lights — our favorite holiday is Thanksgiving.

More than that, though, Thanksgiving is a favorite at our house because it is a holiday that can't be sold.

Nobody exchanges Thanksgiving presents and hardly anybody sends Thanksgiving cards and not too many people go out and buy new wardrobes to wear to Aunt Clara's house for Thanksgiving dinner. Just about the only people who see dollar signs on Thanksgiving are poultry farmers. Department stores ignore it. Television networks can't use it to increase ratings. When it comes to generating income, Thanksgiving is less useful than President's Day.

I didn't always like Thanksgiving best.

Like virtually every other kid, I used to think of Thanksgiving as nothing more than a tuneup for Christmas, a sort of junior varsity game that got us in the mood for the big event. But now Christmas has become the Super Bowl of holidays, an anti-climax that can't possibly live up to all the pre-game hype.

When Santa comes to town on Nov. 15, how do you keep the enthusiasm going until Dec. 25? How many animated Rudolphs and Frostys can you watch before the cuteness begins to stick in your throat like a four-year-old fruitcake? How many *Dolly Parton Christmas Specials* can you endure before the sight of fake stars sitting around fake fireplaces with fake snow falling outside the fake windows behind them makes you begin to suspect that the Grinch had the right idea all along?

Easter is not as crass as Christmas. Still it seems increasingly to be a day owned by discount stores, a day of sugary candy and pink cellophane grass, a day of plastic baskets made in Taiwan and polyester clothes made in Hong Kong. A day in which religious meaning has largely been drowned out by the sound of cash registers.

The Fourth of July, too, is a holiday that seems to have outgrown its roots. No one calls it Independence Day anymore. Now it merely is "the Fourth," a day for fifths and six-packs. A nice enough day, but a day without feeling, without emotion to set it apart from other summer days.

Halloween is a holiday grown ugly, a day upon which costumes come mass-produced and flame-retardent and newspapers run public service stories telling parents where to take their kids' candy to be X-rayed. And New Year's Eve is not a holiday at all, merely an excuse for amateur drinkers, an adults-only evening of false emotions and forced gaiety, followed by a morning of exaggerated hangovers and an afternoon of indistinguishable football games.

But Thanksgiving is none of those things.

Thanksgiving is not a day for kids, nor a day for adults. It is a day for families, a day of driveways filled with cars wearing out-of-state license plates and living rooms filled with aunts and uncles and barely recognizable cousins. Unlike the excitement of Christmas, which begins too early in the morning and lasts only as long as it takes to tear open the final present, Thanksgiving is an all-day anticipation.

It begins the moment the turkey comes out of the refrigerator, pale and clammy, and lasts until the remains return there in plastic wrap, reduced to sandwich filling. In between, it is a day of sounds and smells and warmth. A television turned on, but frequently unheard above the conversations of adults reunited for the day and the clamor of kids reintroduced to cousins they see only once a year. The mingling aromas of pumpkin and cinnamon and yams and, over them all, the essence of turkey, turning slowly, tantalizingly tan. The elbow-to-elbow closeness of a dining room table not quite big enough for all the plates, with not quite enough matching chairs for all the people pulled up to it.

But, if dinner is the focus of Thanksgiving, it is not the ultimate reward. The satisfaction comes later, when conversations grow softer and movement grows slower and simply being together is all that's really important.

That's the way Thanksgiving always has been and it is this reassuring sameness, I think, that makes it the best of all possible holidays. It is the kind of feeling that even the very best store does not —and can not — put on a sales slip.

Which is not to suggest that Thanksgiving is a holiday without challenges. In time the Rockies may tumble and Gibraltar may crumble. But after every Thanksgiving at our house, one thing is there to stay:

Leftover turkey.

I blame part of the problem on poultry farmers. Somehow they got the idea that what America wanted was turkeys with bigger thighs and broader chests. As a result, just about the only turkeys you can find at the supermarket today are built like Romanian shot putters.

But it really doesn't matter what size bird I give to my family. I could serve it a parakeet for Thanksgiving dinner and there still would be leftovers.

It's not as if our kids don't have good appetites. We're talking about four boys to whom Thanksgiving dinner means every potato in Idaho, every cranberry in Rhode Island and enough stuffing to fill the Grand Canyon. But, when it comes to the turkey, one drumstick will last a lifetime.

That could be because none of my kids actually likes turkey. They say they do, but they lie. The only reason they will argue over a drumstick is because they don't want their brothers to have it. But when dinner is finished, a 15-pound turkey will have produced 19 pounds of leftovers.

Food writers spend the entire month of November stuffing their newspaper columns with recipes for leftover turkey guaranteed to please kids. I've tried them all: Turkey *tetrazzini.* Turkey tacos. Turkey pizza. Turkey *a la mode.* I'm not sure who dreams up those recipes, but I'll assure you of one thing: None of them ever met a real child.

I tried one of those recipes one year. It was a recipe for turkey carcass soup. According to the food column, it is a "can't-miss" recipe that will have the kids "clamoring for more."

On the day after Thanksgiving I place the leftover turkey — meat, bones, skin and pop-up thermometer — into a pot, cover it with water, throw in some spices and let it simmer for a few hours. When it is finished, I add some noodles, cook it all a while longer and call the kids to the table.

"What are we having?" one kid asks.

"Soup," I reply.

"What kind?"

"Tur . . . chicken noodle."

"Is it homemade?"

"Of course not. I love you all too much to do that to you. It's straight from the can and I warmed it in the microwave." I don't particularly enjoy lying to my kids, but there's no room for truth when you're trying to sneak leftovers past them.

Satisfied with my story, they begin to eat. All goes well until the first kid finds a sliver of meat in the bottom of his bowl.

"What's this thing?" he demands.

"What does it look like?" I ask.

"Meat."

"Maybe they made a mistake at the soup factory," I try.

"Hey," another kid yells, "here's one in my bowl, too. It looks like . . . "

*"TURKEY!"* they scream in unison. *"IT'S LEFTOVER TURKEY FROM THANKSGIVING."*

Three kid suffer major injuries in the scramble to spit mouthfuls of turkey soup into the kitchen sink.

Since then, I haven't even tried to slip leftovers into my kids. On Thanksgiving evening I merely take the leftover turkey, wrap it in foil and stuff it into the back of the refrigerator. When the breast is petrified and the drumsticks are hard enough for Jose Canseco to hit home runs with, I will take the remains of the eternal turkey and throw them away.

That will be in mid-December. Usually on the same day we receive the first perpetual fruitcake.

For a blended family, though, there probably is no more complicated holiday than Mother's Day.

Mother's Day used to be a warm and simple affair.

On the second Saturday in May, every kid in America would get on his bike and ride to the nearest five-and-dime store with two weeks worth of paper route savings in his pocket.

There he would buy a box of candy that had been left over since Valentine's Day, a potted plant that would die before Memorial Day or a bottle of cheap cologne that would wind up in the back of a closet until it was thrown out shortly after Labor Day.

But it was, of course, the thought that counted. And on the second Sunday in May, every mother in America who received her tribute would declare herself to be the luckiest Mom in the world.

Those were less complicated days, a Norman Rockwellian era in which the term "blended family" had not yet been invented and the typical American household included 2.3 children and 1.0 mothers.

It's not that way anymore. Now mothers come in three categories: Yours, mine and "that woman Dad married." And shopping for Mother's Day presents is more confusing than the latest simplified income tax form. For us, the complications begin when my stepsons come home from school on the first Monday in May.

"You guys didn't forget about Mother's Day, did you?" I ask them. It is not really a question. Especially in the case of the 15-year-old, who didn't know about Christmas last year until Dec. 29.

"I know what I'm going to get her," says the 12-year-old. "Will you drive us to the mall?"

"Sure," I agree. "On the way, we'll pick up your stepbrothers and they can get something for their mom, too."

"Are they going to get something for our mom?"

"Uh, to tell the truth, I hadn't really thought about that," I admit. "But I guess so, sure. After all, she is their stepmother."

I load my stepsons into the car, drive to my ex-wife's house, pick up my sons, drive to my stepsons' father's house so they can hit him up for some money and proceed to the mall.

"OK, you guys," I announce. "If we do this right, we can get the whole thing over with in 30 minutes. The 12-year-old goes with the 15-year-old to get a present for their mom. The 14-year-old goes with the 17-year-old to get two presents, one for their mom and one for their stepmother. Then we'll all meet back here at 6:30."

"What about our stepmother?" asks her 15-year-old.

"Who?"

"Our dad's wife."

"Oh, of course. I guess you need to buy something for her, too."

"Do we have to buy her something?" my 14-year-old wants to know.

"Well, I'm pretty sure you're not related, but just to be safe, maybe you should . . . "

"Wait a minute," her 15-year-old says to my 14-year-old. "If you buy something for her, that means we'd have to buy something for your mother."

"You've never even met my mother."

"Yes I have. She's tall and she has brown hair."

"That's *your* mother."

"No it isn't. My mother is short and . . . "

After 15 minutes of "Name That Mother," we finally decide on a course of action. They are going to pool their money, buy half a gallon of the cheapest cologne on the market, divide it equally into fruit jars and hand them to the first three women they see on Sunday morning.

Which may not be exactly the way Norman Rockwell painted it. But it's a lot different now that there are 2.3 mothers for every kid in America.

I guess it's not much easier for our kids on Father's Day. Because, no matter how many fathers you have, finding a suitable present for him is nearly impossible.

To be honest, fathers don't make it easy. Sometimes, when my kids ask, "What do you want for Father's Day?" I tell them that if they really love me they will combine their allowances and buy me a Mercedes convertible. Red. With wire wheels.

But most fathers, I'm pretty sure, answer it the way my father always did.

"Aw, save your money," he would say every year. "I don't really need anything."

Which was true, of course. What could a kid of 12 afford that a grown man didn't already own if he really wanted it? Still, it is not a very satisfying answer to a kid who has learned that the way we show love in our society is to buy things for other people.

One problem with fathers is that few of us have learned to be gracious receivers. Our roles have been to give gifts, not to accept them, and we are uncomfortable opening the presents that our wives and children hand us. Perhaps it is a threat to the image we have of ourselves as providers, as if accepting a gift somehow threatens our masculinity.

Then again, all of that my be feminist psychological claptrap and maybe the real reason we don't like to get gifts from our families is because we know it's probably something dumb we wouldn't actually pay for ourselves, but it's going to appear on our credit card bill next month, anyway.

Whatever the reason, finding a gift for a father is a lot harder than finding one for a mother. Mothers love anything you ever give them. Or at least they say they do. You could pick up a rock in the backyard, paint it green, put it in a sandwich bag and hand it to your mother and she will carry on as if you had given her a 72-carat emerald.

It's almost impossible to buy the wrong gift for your mother. She likes bouquets and potted plants, candy and perfume. She likes breakfast in bed and she likes going out for dinner. She likes expensive jewelry and she likes things made out of construction paper and magic marker. She likes clothes. She likes practical things for the kitchen and she likes useless little ceramic figurines that sit on a shelf and beg for someone to come along and knock them off with a Nerf football.

For your father, on the other hand, you can shop all month and you're probably not going to find anything that won't spend the rest of its life on the back of his closet shelf.

Part of the problem is that most men aren't into trinkets. The toys of manhood generally are big ticket items such as power boats and power tools, pool tables and motorcycles.

The advertisers aren't much help. Their idea of a perfect Father's Day gift is a lawn mower. Which is pretty much like buying a vacuum cleaner for Mother's Day. Probably the worst television commercial I've seen in years suggested that what your father really wants is rented furniture.

Most of the Fathers Day ads I see in newspapers are for aftershave or reclining chairs. Maybe that says something about the way we picture our fathers: Guys who sit on their butts all day and smell bad.

The worst fathers of all to buy for are the ones who don't have any hobbies or any interest in sports. The only reason I play tennis is so my kids will be able to go out and buy me wristbands or a can of balls whenever it's Father's Day, Christmas or my birthday.

Which doesn't mean I won't tell my children how much I appreciate the wristbands or the tennis balls or the coffee cup with the annoyingly cute saying on it that they get me each Father's Day. I will thank them profusely and smile while they are taking my picture and do my best to act as if Father's Day is the highlight of my year.

But the truth is, if there never was another Father's Day, if there never was another Father's Day gift, it would not change what I feel for them. Because they have already, each of them in their own way, given me a lifetime of gifts.

They have given me a sense of responsibility.

For a man, a baby brings with it a feeling of purpose that comes only with knowing that you have been entrusted with the care of another human being. It was, at first, a frightening, intimidating feeling. But as they grew, my self-assurance grew with them. Their well-being was proof to the world of my maturity. It was, more importantly, proof to myself.

They have given me laughter.

Kids do not always say the darndest things. But they do have a way of looking at the absurdities of life in the adult world that the most talented satirist can only imitate.

They have given me tears.

They are not always bad things, tears. But I didn't know that for a long time and so I fought manfully against them. Until the day I saw my oldest child in a wedding gown and my youngest child in a tuxedo. That day I cried because she looked so young and because he looked so old and because I realized, for the first time, that fatherhood was not forever, after all. And I discovered, with those tears, what mothers always have known: If you do not cry for your children, you are not taking the job personally enough.

They have given me pride and satisfaction. Memories and fulfillment.

What have I done in my life, what *could* I do in my life, that will match the pride of watching one son score his first touchdown in a high school football game and the satisfaction of seeing another sink the winning free throw in a junior high basketball game? There are few moments in my career as memorable as the moment a stepson walked out into the spotlight on an elementary school stage, a 12-year-old Ebenezer Scrooge in *A Christmas Carol.* Journalism doesn't offer an award as fulfilling as the applause I heard when my other stepson sat on a stage with his high school rock band and sang words that came from his heart.

They have given me hope.

With each year it becomes increasingly possible that I will not find the cure for cancer, write the great American novel or hit the game winner in the bottom of the ninth at Yankee Stadium. But my children give me another generation of chances. They are my best shot at immortality.

There is nothing my kids can give me on Father's Day that could equal all that.

Anyway, you don't have kids so they can give you gifts.

Kids *are* gifts.

# ADAM

On a hazy summer morning, while other parents worked and other children played, we buried our son.

He was only 16.

There were four parents there to grieve. A mother. A father. A stepmother. A stepfather. Four parents there to share the numbness and the pain that a senseless, incomprehensible fall from a bridge had brought to them.

He had come latest into my life, just a little more than three years earlier. There had been not enough time to know him as well as the others knew him. Not enough time to build the bond that the others had forged. Not enough time.

But just a little more than three years was enough for me to learn to love him.

He was such an easy kid to love.

He was funny and bright and a little bit goofy. He was everything a 16-year-old boy should be.

And on a hazy summer morning, while other parents worked and other children played, I grasped at the straws of memories to help myself through the pain.

All the memories were good.

There had been six children in my life and this was the only one to whom I had never really raised my voice in anger. There never had been a need.

He was a kid who was eager to please, eager to make other people happy. He was, everyone who met him said, a sweet kid. There was no more fitting description.

He was smart. The school report cards told us that. But, as smart as he was, he never seemed to be able to remember phone messages. If we had gotten a call from Gorbachev, all he would have been able to tell us was, "Some guy named Mike called. I think he was from out of town."

He loved soccer and practiced for long hours to win a spot on the reserve team. But no matter how hard he worked at developing his physical coordination, he never mastered the art of keeping a napkin on his lap. After a while we gave up and whoever set the table for dinner just threw his napkin on the floor.

Music was his other passion. He spent slightly more than an eternity each day practicing his guitar in his bedroom and he talked endlessly about the name of the band he was going to form with his buddies. They settled on "Peace Cows." The name didn't make much sense. But it didn't *not* make much sense, either.

In the spring, there was a talent show at the high school. "'Peace Cows" won first place and a check for $100. He put the check into his pocket and borrowed money from his father to go out and celebrate at Friendly's.

He was ambitious and knew what he wanted to do with his life. He was going to move to Colorado and open a record store. Or a car wash. Or, maybe, a combination record store and car wash. A lot depended on when you talked with him about it.

He fell in love a lot, sometimes more than once a day. We had given up trying to keep track of the names.

Although he got along pretty well with his stepbrothers, he argued with his little brother nearly as often as he fell in love. But he was the one with the biggest grin when his little brother turned 13 and his family surprised him with an electric guitar for his birthday.

That's how he was. Funny and bright and just a little goofy. But, most of all, sweet.

His name was Adam.

I was not his father.

But he was my son.

# CHAPTER 14

# OOOOOOO OOOOOOO

He was 13 when we met. We got along from the very first belch.

Five minutes after we are introduced, he rips one to see if he can shock me. I rip one back to show him that he can't, because I already have been through two 13-year-old boys. Our relationship is "cool" from then on.

To keep it that way, I make a point of showing that I am interested in his activities. When he is in his soccer stage and wants to talk about headers and penalty kicks, I listen and nod my head, even though I think the only thing less exciting than watching soccer is hearing about soccer. When he is in his music mode and talks endlessly about the virtues of Jerry Garcia, I listen and nod my head, even though the only Garcia I ever heard of used to be a pitcher for the Cleveland Indians.

I even go to his home economics class with him.

They didn't have home economics for boys when I was in school. When I was in school, boys took manly courses that would prepare them to be manly men. Courses like mechanical drawing. And shop. Only girls took courses that taught cooking and sewing. Apparently it never occured to the educators of my day that a man might eventually find himself in a shirt that did not have a button. Or in a kitchen that did not come equipped with a woman.

Not that the manly courses I took were a total waste. In shop I learned how to make a garden trowel and a lamp. Training like that is not to be taken lightly. Of course, I've never actually been faced with the need to make a garden trowel since I graduated from high school. But you never know.

Education today is different. At the risk of losing this country's world leadership in garden trowel making, schools have opened the kitchen doors to boys.

I learn about this development in American education when his mother calls me at work shortly before noon one day.

"How would you like to have a free lunch?" she asks.

"Sounds great," I answer.

"Fine. Be at the 13-year-old's school at 1:45. Today's the day his home economics class invites parents to taste what the kids have cooked. I can't get off work in time, but I knew you'd want to be there." She hangs up before I can tell her exactly how much I want to be there.

At 1:45 I find myself in a classroom filled with ovens, sinks, 13-year-old giggling gourmets and an assortment of other parents who apparently couldn't come up with a good excuse, either.

Displayed on a long table is a variety of dishes created in the home economics class. I locate the 13-year-old who belongs to me every other week and we carry our paper plates to the line at the serving table.

"What did you contribute to this smorgasbord?" I ask him.

"Spicy sugar cookies and jalapeno chip dip."

"An interesting concept in *nouvelle cuisine*," I comment. "Most people aren't adventurous enough to dip their cookies into anything but milk."

"The jalapeno dip isn't for the cookies," he says. "It's for taco chips. They're two separate dishes."

"I knew that," I tell him. Actually, I only *hoped* that. I have, after all, seen the 13-year-old eat.

When we reach the serving table, I take a small sample from each dish.

"Leave room for my cookies," the 13-year-old urges.

"Where are they?"

"Right there. Next to the taco chips."

"Which is which?"

"The cookies don't have salt on them."

I pick up one of the cookies he has made. It is approximately the thickness of medium-gauge aluminum foil. It is the first cookie I ever have seen that could give you a paper cut.

"Do you think they're too thin?" the 13-year-old asks.

"Not at all," I assure him. "I've always preferred cookies I could see through."

"Maybe I used too much baking powder."

"How much did you use?"

"A tablespoonful," he says. "Or maybe it was a cupful. I forget. Anyway, at least they turned out better than the first batch."

"There was a first batch?"

"They caught on fire."

I take a bite of the anorexic cookie in my hand. Despite its build, it doesn't taste all that bad. Still, it might not be a bad idea if the kid learned how to make a garden trowel.

As he heads into his 14th summer, he puts away his mixing bowls and begins to plan how he will spend his vacation.

With the other three kids, there is no question.

The 16-year-old is going to waste all three months lounging around shopping malls, pizza places and other teen-age hangouts. The 13-year-old plans to idle away the summer at the playground shooting baskets and developing a vocabulary like Eddie Murphy's. On the day school lets out, the 11-year-old will sit down in front of the television with his Nintendo controls. He will not stand up again until Labor Day.

But we worry about the 14-year-old. He wants to spend the summer working.

I try to discourage him. I remind him of the joys of watching MTV until 3 in the morning and not getting up the next day until after noon. I point out that the swim club is bound to be overrun by teen-age girls who will be devoting their summers to testing the local indecent exposure laws.

But I can't get through to the kid. He is determined to blow an entire summer making money.

"I've got it all figured out," he enthuses. "Me and my buddy Graham are going to make almost a thousand bucks this summer. Me and him got this plan. And guess what I'm going to do with the money?"

"Hire an English tutor?"

"Nah. I'm gonna get me this humongous amplifier for my guitar. It's a real monster. When you crank it up you can feel your eardrums swelling up inside your head until the wax starts dripping down your . . . "

"I'm sure I can't wait for that experience," I interrupt. "But just how are you going to make this thousand dollars?"

"Mowing lawns."

"You're planning to make a thousand bucks mowing lawns?"

"You don't think we can make that much?"

"Not unless the lawn is in front of the White House."

"Me and Graham have it all figured out. We're going to print up flyers and pass them out all over the city. If we only sign up 15 customers at $10 a yard, that's $900 for the summer right there."

"Assuming you get 15 customers, that's going to keep you awfully busy," I warn. "You're going to have to average more than two lawns a day, seven days a week."

"We're only going to cut them every other week."

"What are your customers supposed to do between mowings, swing through their yards on vines?"

"What do you mean?"

"What I mean is, lawn mowing is not the same as washing your hair. You've got to do it more than twice a month. Not only is that going to keep you pretty busy, it's going to put quite a strain on Graham's mower."

"Graham doesn't have a mower."

"Neither do we," I remind him. "So how did you plan on cutting these lawns, with a rented goat?"

"Well, we thought if you could lend us $500 or so, we could buy a mower and then pay you back. It doesn't have to be a real big mower. In fact, it has to be small enough to fit in the back of your car. Our customers' yards might be so far apart you'll have to drive us to them."

"Let me see if I'm catching the drift here," I summarize. "You expect me to cough up $500 so you can buy a lawn mower that will drip oil on the backseat of my car while I spend seven days a week driving you and your friend from customer to customer?"

"You're right, that's a bad plan," he concedes. "You'll have to lend us enough money to buy a trailer, too."

Like most of the plans of most of my kids, the great summer vacation lawn mowing bonanza never quite cuts it and he spends the summer unemployed, unaware, and, as nearly as I can tell, unconscious.

His sudden lapse into a universe that is not necessarily parallel to ours seems to surprise his mother a great deal more than it surprises me. Even though we both brought teen-age boys to our second marriages, we have vastly different perceptions of them. She tends to regard them as girls with fuzzy upper lips. She keeps assuming they are aware, sensitive, concerned human beings. I think she's wrong on all four counts.

Having lived through a teen-age boyhood of my own, I see teen-age boys for what they really are: lobotomized zombies who lurch through adolescence leaving lights on, doors open and toilet seats up. It's not that teen-age boys don't care about the world around them. It's just that they haven't noticed there is one.

The difference in the way we view teen-age boys comes into focus when she arrives home one day carrying a large shopping bag.

"What's in the bag?' I ask.

"Sheets and pillow cases for the 14-year-old's bedroom," she replies. "He's going to love them."

"Hah."

"What does that mean?"

"Teen-age boys do not love sheets and pillow cases," I explain to her. "Teen-age boys love Mopeds, cars, loud music, loud teen-age girls and burning school buildings."

"Maybe that's the way your kids are," she counters. "But my 14-year-old happens to be very appreciative of the things I do to make his surroundings more attractive."

She goes up the 14-year-old's room to put the new sheets and pillow cases on his bed. A few hours later the 14-year-old comes home, heads up to his room and closes the door. The next time we see him is at the dinner table.

Expectantly, his mother waits for him to mention the sheets and pillow cases. Fourteen tacos later, the subject still has not come up. Finally, she can't stand it.

"Don't you love the sheets?" she asks him.

"Sheets?" he replies.

"The new ones on your bed."

"Bed?" he replies.

"That's the thing you hide your Victoria's Secret catalogs under," I translate.

The 14-year-old turns to look at me.

"Who are you?" he asks.

"I'm your stepfather."

"My mom got remarried?"'

"A year and a half ago."

"Cool. Pass the salsa."

A few months later, she tries again to prove that he is conscious.

In exchange for seven or eight years' salary, contractors have come in to redecorate our kitchen. They install new counters, a new double sink, an instant-hot faucet and tiles on the wall. As a bonus to show how much they appreciate our business, they throw in a new rubber sink stopper at no extra charge.

"The kitchen looks wonderful," my wife exclaims when it is finished. "The 14-year-old is going to be impressed."

That afternoon the 14-year-old comes home from school. He walks directly to the kitchen to prepare himself a snack.

He does not notice.

He reappears in the kitchen a few hours later for dinner.

He does not notice.

After dinner he washes the dishes.

He does not notice.

At 10 o'clock that night he returns to the kitchen for another snack. We are sitting in the living room when we hear his voice.

"Hey, cool," he says. "We got a new sink stopper."

His mother looks at me, obviously discouraged by his reaction. I, on the other hand, look at it as progress. He is right on course for the "foggy fifteens."

Parents who think they have won the child-raising war because they have survived the "terrible twos" are in for a major shock when they reach the "foggy fifteens." There probably is no scientific explanation for this phenomenon. But, trust me, it is as much a part of adolescence as rock music, long phone calls and eternal showers.

One day you have a reasonably alert 14-year-old. The next thing you know, his brain shuts down completely and he disappears into a fog from which he might not emerge until midway through his junior year in college.

Intelligence has nothing to do with it. A 15-year-old can be getting straight A's in high school. In history class he can memorize the dates of every major war in Western civilization. But on the morning of Dec. 25 he will walk into the living room and ask, "What's that tree doing in here?"

I have walked through the fog with three different kids, none of whom remembers a minute of it.

One kid spent his entire 15th year falling down stairways. It wasn't until he turned 16 that we discovered he had been wearing his contact lenses in the wrong eyes.

Even in its mildest form, the "foggy fifteens" is a trip through the Twilight Zone. You can almost hear the spooky music in the background and Rod Serling saying, "There is a fifth dimension beyond that which is known to man. It is a dimension as vast as space and as timeless as infinity. On the day they turn 15, boys disappear into this dimension."

Not long after her son stumbles into this foggy universe, we are in the living room. I am reading the newspaper. He is watching MTV. His mother is putting on her coat.

"I'm going to the grocery store," she announces. "I'll be back in about an hour."

"Bye," she says, kissing me.

"Bye," I say.

"Bye," she says, kissing the 15-year-old.

"Bye," he says.

She leaves. Twelve seconds later the phone rings. The 15-year-old answers it.

"MOM," he yells, "it's for you."

I stare at him for a moment or two, hoping that even one tiny point of light will penetrate the fog. But there is no sign of intelligent life coming from the vicinity of the 15-year-old's world.

"Your mother's not here," I finally inform him.

"She isn't?"

"Take my word for it."

"When did she leave?"

"Three seconds after she kissed you goodbye."

"Where did she go?"

"To the grocery store."

"When will she be back?"

"In about an hour."

"Oh."

He gets up and walks out of the room, leaving the television blasting, his shoes on the couch, the telephone off the hook and the person at the other end hanging on.

Ten minutes later he returns.

"Where's my mom?" he asks.

"I don't know," I tell him. "The last I saw of her, she was riding away on the back of some guy's motorcycle with a rose between her teeth and all her hair shaved off."

I turn back to my newspaper and wait for this information to penetrate through the fog. Five minutes later, he asks:

"What kind of motorcycle?"

Airports have been closed down by less fog than that.

But even when they are shrouded by impenetrable clouds, teen-agers are not terribly complicated creatures. To be a successful parent of a teen-ager, it helps to remember a basic rule:

*Whatever you assume about your teen-ager will be wrong.*

If you fix a dinner you "know" your teen-ager will love — pizza, tacos, hot dogs and french fries — he will look up from his plate and ask, "Don't we have any beets?"

If you buy him a CD with the greatest hits of the Grateful Dead, Guns n' Roses, Paula Abdul and Megadeath, he will toss it into a desk drawer and say, "Nice. But what I really was hoping for was a Barry Manilow album."

There is no way to predict what a teen-ager will like. This is because teen-agers do not know what they will like until after you have told them what you don't like. In the chess game of parenthood, you never get the last move.

To a teen-ager, there is only one test to determine what is cool: Cool is anything that makes a parent's eyes roll back into his or her skull. Ultimate cool is anything that makes a parent pass out.

As a veteran of three previous teen-agers, I probably should have explained all that to my wife when her first teen-ager comes downstairs en route to his first big date.

It is a date about which he has been talking all week. Not only is this date with the "coolest girl in school," it is possible she is the coolest girl who ever walked the hallway of any school that ever existed.

His mother, naturally, figures he is going to get pretty duded up for an event this momentous. While he is in the shower, she lays out his best clothes: A blue blazer, gray slacks, blue oxford-cloth Polo shirt, Armani tie and cordovan loafers. In this outfit, she says, he will look like he stepped off the cover of *GQ*.

An hour and a half later he is out of the shower and getting dressed. We know he is getting dressed, because the walls are vibrating from the noise coming out of his CD player. The 15-year-old cannot get dressed without the help of loud music. If his CD player breaks down some morning, he will have to go to school naked.

Eventually he comes downstairs. He is not wearing any of the clothes his mother laid out for him. He is wearing a wrinkled red sweatshirt with the bottom of a white T-shirt sticking out beneath it, Bermuda shorts, tube socks and a pair of shower clogs. He does not look like he stepped off the cover of *GQ*. He looks like he stepped off the cover of *Bag Ladies Monthly*.

"I thought you had a date tonight," his mother says when her eyes have stopped rolling back into her head.

"I do," he answers.

"Well, don't you think you'd better get dressed for it?"

"What do you mean?" he demands. "Don't you think this outfit is cool?"

"Of course we do," I assure him. "It's just that we didn't know you were going to a Madonna lookalike contest. Have a good time."

"Thanks," he says, clunking out the door in his shower clogs. While the door still is rattling, I head for the bathroom to find the smelling salts. I blame myself for not having prepared her for this moment.

The next time he has a date, I will suggest to her that she lay out a torn T-shirt, boxer shorts, suspenders, argyle socks and tennis shoes with holes in the toes. If I know anything at all about teen-agers, the kid will walk out the door wearing a three-piece Brooks Brothers suit and wing-tip shoes.

Somehow as he is drifting through the fog, he finds enough money to buy an electric guitar. I'm not sure what it cost. I'm not sure what kind it is. I'm not even sure how many strings it has. Just about the only thing I know about electric guitars is what I picked up watching *The Partridge Family*.

*The Partridge Family* was one of television's major contributions to Western culture in the early '70s. It was a weekly spellbinder about a widow and her houseful of revoltingly wholesome kids, all of whom performed together as a rock music group.

It never was clear to me how Mrs. Partridge became a widow. After watching the show a few times, I just sort of assumed the late Mr. Partridge expired from a saccharine overdose.

Now I have a different theory. I don't think he's even dead. I think he's just trapped somewhere in their house under a pile of amplifiers.

The amplifier theory occurs to me when I come home from work and find the 15-year-old sitting on the living room couch. At least I assume he is sitting on the couch. It's impossible to be sure, because the spot in the living room where I remember the couch being when I left for work that morning is chin high in guitars, guitar cases, guitar picks, electrical wires, amplifiers and speakers.

"When did the roadies leave?" I ask him.

"What roadies are those?"

"Well, the only explanation I can think of for all this stuff is that The Rolling Stones have added our house to their reunion tour and they had their equipment delivered here in advance."

"Nah, this is just my stuff," he says.

"You're kidding. The Philharmonic could perform the collected works of Mozart with less equipment than this."

"Phil who?"

"Never mind. The question is, what is all this stuff doing in the living room and when are the moving men coming to get it out of here?"

"We had to bring our stuff down here so we'd have room to practice," he says.

"We?"

"Yeah. Me and the 14-year-old. We're gonna start a band."

"A band of what?"

"You know. A rock band."

"You mean like the Beatles?"

"Sort of. Only we'll play real music."

They have it all figured out, he explains. They're going to think up a name, learn some songs and go on tour. Not necessarily in that order. While he is assuring me that they are really serious about this and are committed to becoming a monster success, even if it takes several weekends, an amplifier roughly the size of the World Trade Center staggers down the stairs.

"I could use a little help," wheezes a voice from behind the amplifier. The voice belongs to the 14-year-old. He lurches into the living room. Before I can help him, he drops the amplifier on a table in the corner of the room. There is a cracking sound and the amplifier slides slowly across the table top in the direction of the broken leg. They don't make circa 1780 tilt-top Chippendale tables like they used to.

While I go to look for the glue gun, the 14-year-old brings down the rest of his equipment. By the time I return, the living room has been transformed into a Radio Shack warehouse.

They flip the switches on their guitars and begin to rehearse. The speakers produce enough noise to lower your IQ. I climb over an amplifier, scale a speaker, fight my way through a jungle of electric cords and go upstairs to look for ear plugs. As I open the bedroom door, I find my wife just hanging up the telephone.

"Who were you talking to?" I shout.

"Someone who was calling to complain about the noise," she yells.

"One of the neighbors?" I scream.

"I don't know who it was. But they were calling long distance," she hollers. "Maybe you'd better go back downstairs and tell them to turn down their amplifiers."

Not a chance. That's probably the line Mrs. Partridge used to get rid of her old man.

Nobody ever said that getting through the stepfather game with your sanity, or even with your hearing, would be easy. But I keep working at it.

When I assign household chores, which is seldom, I assign them equally to my kids and to her kids. When the household chores don't get done, which is often, I yell equally at my kids and at her kids. I am an equal-opportunity nagger.

Sometimes, when I am forced to discipline my kids, I discipline her kids, too, even if they haven't done anything wrong. I don't want any of them to feel neglected.

That's why I feel sort of bad about missing the 15-year-old's soccer season.

As I may have mentioned, soccer is not my favorite sport, even though millions of people seem to love it. The difference between me and them, I guess, is that they actually understand the game.

All I know about soccer is that a bunch of people in short pants and tall socks run around a field kicking each other in the shins and once a month or so the ball accidentally goes into the goal. I prefer American football, where a bunch of people in plastic hats run around a field butting each other on the head and once a month or so one of them accidentally falls into the end zone with the ball in his hands.

But when her 15-year-old announces that he is going out for the reserve soccer team, I copy the season schedule into my appointment book, buy extra film for my camera and rearrange my calendar to make sure I won't miss any of his games.

The first game of the season, according to the schedule I have copied into my book, is on a Wednesday at 7 p.m. I take my camera and drive to the soccer field. When I arrive at the stadium, I see a bunch of people running around on the field, kicking each other in the shins. None of the kickers, or the kickees, is my stepson. Finally, though, I spot him. He is the one sitting in the stands with three cheerleaders.

"Why are you sitting in the stands with three cheerleaders?" I ask him.

"Must be my sex appeal," he replies.

"What I mean is, why aren't you out there on the field kicking somebody in the shins?"

"Our game is over," he says. "This is the varsity game."

I glance at my watch. It says 7:04.

"What did you play, a pair of two-minute halves?"

"Our game started at 5:30."

"The schedule says 7."

"It got changed. We had to play at 5:30 so the varsity could start at 7."

Suddenly, the lessons learned through years of experience as a sports father come rushing back to me. The very first lesson I learned was: Never trust a school schedule for any sports activity beneath the varsity level.

It doesn't matter if the schedule has been drawn up by the faculty of the Harvard law school and notarized by the Supreme Court. It is not binding. I don't care if the schedule has been brought down from a mountain top by a guy in sandals and a robe. By the middle of the season it will not be worth the stone tablets it is written on.

With that lesson in mind, I try again the following week. The schedule says 5 p.m. I show up at 4 p.m. The 15-year-old is not on the field or in the stands. The field is empty. The stands are empty. The only person in sight is a groundskeeper. He is not kicking anyone in the shins.

"Isn't there supposed to be a soccer game here tonight?" I ask him.

"I think it got switched to the other team's field."

I drive to the other team's field. Which is in a different time zone. As I pull into the parking lot, the 15-year-old's team bus passes me. It is pulling out of the parking lot. I have missed another game.

The next week's game is scheduled for Tuesday, a day upon which I am supposed to be out of town for business. I rearrange my schedule so that I will be out of town on Monday, instead. On Tuesday morning, just to be sure that the site or the time of the game hasn't been changed, I call the school's athletic office. Even the dumbest stepfather can be taught new tricks.

"When and where, exactly, is tonight's reserve soccer game?" I ask.

"Oh," a woman says, "they played that game yesterday. The referees had a scheduling conflict."

I wind up missing the 15-year-old's entire season. And I could kick myself for it. In the shins.

When he turns 16, the fog lifts just long enough for him to pass his driver's license test. It is a big milestone for him. And an even bigger one for me. It is the opportunity to get a few miles back.

When you are a parent, you measure the length of your parenthood in different ways. Some measure it in terms of years already served and years remaining until the last kid is out the door. Others calculate it on the basis of school open houses attended, tennis shoes purchased or slumber parties survived.

I measure parenthood by the mile.

As nearly as I can estimate, my cars and I have rolled up roughly 500,000 miles en route to soccer practices, music lessons, orthodontist's appointments and after-dinner trips back to school to visit lockers containing homework assignments that absolutely, positively have to be finished before tomorrow morning. When a kid gets a driver's license, a parent has a chance to roll back the odometer.

Of course, like most of parenthood, it's a longshot. But I give it a try one day when my current free taxi is in the repair shop, undergoing treatment for exhaustion. Since the 16-year-old has his license and access to a car, I figure he can drive to my office after school and give me a ride home. After all the miles I have spent on him, it's the least he can do.

That morning I hand the 16-year-old a list of detailed instructions on how to get from his school to my office. The instructions begin:

"Open the car door on the driver's side. Get into the car. Sit down. Close the car door." When you're dealing with a 16-year-old, you don't take anything for granted. It's not that he is unintelligent. But the fog tends to come and go.

At 3:30, I finish work, leave the office and stand on the sidewalk in front of the building to wait for the 16-year-old to pick me up. At 3:35 I spot the front end of his car coming down the street. At 3:36, I spot the rear end of his car going up the street.

Because my office building is surrounded by one-way signs, my guess is that, by the time he realizes his mistake and finds his way back, he will be approaching the side of the building. Of course, there is always a chance that, by the time he realizes his mistake he will be somewhere in Kansas. But I'm hoping for the best. As I walk to the side of the building to wait for his second attempt, it occurs to me that it probably would have been faster to take the bus home.

Ten minutes later I spot him coming down the street that runs alongside the building. I begin waving my arms to attract his attention. By the time he sees me, he is even with the building. In the wrong lane. And slightly less than seven inches ahead of the semi that is on his rear bumper. Making one of his better decisions, the 16-year-old chooses not to slam on the brakes.

His taillights disappear around the corner. As I head back to wait at the front of the building, it occurs to me that it probably would have been faster to walk home. On my hands.

Fifteen minutes later, on his third approach, he finally makes a four-point landing. He pulls up in front of the building. I open the door and hop in.

"We seemed to have had a little trouble making connections there," I observe.

"Yeah," he says. "How about giving me some bucks?"

"What for?"

"To pay for the gas I had to use getting here. You don't expect me to drive all over town for you for nothing, do you?"

That's how he was. Funny and sweet and just a little bit goofy.

I'm not sure if he knew I loved him. I hope so. Of course, that might be asking too much. Maybe I should just be satisfied with telling myself that at least he knew I was the guy who married his mom.

Probably.

PREFACE: CHAPTER 15

# STEPTEENS

After three years of marriage, the youngest kid in our house becomes a teen-ager. It is a milestone that carries with it the inescapable message that I am aging.

But getting older doesn't bother me. What bothers me is that I will be getting dumber.

Again.

Based on my research of five previous teen-agers, I have managed to formulate a mathematical equation that covers what is about to happen to me: A parent's intellectual abilities diminish in direct proportion to the maturation of his or her children.

In other words, the older they get, the dumber you get. Before your kid reaches 19, your IQ will reach zero.

Not every kid is exactly alike, of course. But if this one approaches teen-agehood the way the other ones did, these are some of the things that will happen around our house during the next seven years:

One day I will walk, unannounced, into his bedroom. The haze of smoke hanging over his bed will resemble a Los Angeles still-life.

"Has someone in here been smoking?" I will ask him.

"Why (cough, cough)? What makes you think anybody in here's been smoking? There's probably (choke, wheeze) something wrong with the furnace."

One evening we will have friends at our house for drinks and dinner. I will prepare a vodka on the rocks for one of them. He will sip it and say something like, "I didn't know you could get Perrier-flavored vodka around here." I will taste the vodka and discover that its alcohol content is roughly 12-proof.

The next day I will confront the resident teen-age bartender.

"I think someone has been sampling my vodka and replacing it with water in an attempt to fool his stepfather," I will say.

"Now that you mention it, I did notice the cat staggering through the kitchen last night," he will answer.

At the end of a grading period, we will receive a report card indicating that our teen-age scholar has missed 46 of the last 48 school days. We will ask him about it.

"I was there every day," he will swear. "The teacher just couldn't see me when she was taking attendance because the kid who sits at the desk in front of me is the center on the basketball team."

Shortly after he turns 16, our teen-age driver will borrow the car "to go to the library," which is three blocks from our house.

The next time I see the car, it will have 163 new miles on the odometer, an eyedropper's worth of gas in the tank, four pounds of empty soft drink cans in the back seat and footprints on the ceiling.

I will lead him to the garage and point out these things.

"Oh my gosh," he will say, "someone must have broken into the car while I was studying in the reference section."

When he reaches the vicinity of 17, he will come home with a friend of the opposite gender. They will go to the basement "to study." An hour later, I will walk down the basement stairs. Their books will be stacked on the floor. They will be stacked on the couch. Joined at the lips.

"It's a CPR course," he will explain.

Fortunately, I know that the lowering of my IQ is only a temporary condition and that, in approximately seven years, it will return to normal.

Of course, by that time it will be too late.

# CHAPTER 15

# OOOOOOOOOOOOOOOOO

If there's anything my plunge into the icy lake of stepfatherhood has proved to me, it's that there are no real differences between teen-agers. Stepteen-agers are exactly like your original teen-agers. They just came into the world with different last names.

And they all are equally guilty of the same seven deadly teen-age sins:

**ARGUMENTATIVENESS**

Every few years there seems to be a big fuss about picking a new Supreme Court justice.

I don't understand why. The answer is obvious. If they really want the most qualified person for the job, all they have to do is appoint any parent who has raised two or more kids.

If it is nothing else, parenthood is 18 years of playing Solomon. A lifetime of hearing arguments and appeals. Nothing that comes before the Supreme Court is likely to be any tougher than deciding whether the kid who has to take out the garbage is getting an easier job than the kid who has to set the dinner table. You think affirmative action is a tough issue? Try dividing two Popsicles among three kids.

Compared to parents, Supreme Court justices have it easy. At least the arguments they hear aren't being presented to them by two kids who are screaming at the top of their lungs while they punch each other's shoulders.

I put on my black robe and hear oral arguments approximately a dozen times a day. Sometimes the cases are as complex as an anti-trust suit. Like the one that begins with a casual comment from my bench partner, who emerges from the bathroom with a toilet brush in one hand, a spray bottle of porcelain cleaner in the other and demands:

"When did I become the maid around here?"

"Are you just making conversation with that question, or were you actually looking for a specific date?" I ask.

"It's not a question at all," she snaps. "It's a warning. This is the third bathroom I've cleaned today and I'm sick of it. There needs to be a better division of labor around here."

"You're absolutely right," I agree. "Instead of cleaning them all in one day, you should divide them up. You could clean the downstairs bathroom on Saturdays, the kids' bathroom on Tuesd. . . "

The rest of my advice is interrupted by a flying toilet brush, which could have inflicted some pretty noticeable damage to the side of my head if she had better aim.

"You're upset, aren't you?" I inquire. Like most husbands of the 90s, I have learned to understand even the most subtle, non-verbal communications from my mate.

"Upset? Why should I be upset? What more could a woman want than to spend the day cleaning toilets, mopping floors and doing laundry while her family sits around on their big fat . . . "

"I think I'm starting to see where you're going with this. I suppose I could be a little more helpful around the house. And so could the kids. We're just going to have to assign chores. No big deal."

Which is, of course, simply the latest in a long line of bad decisions I have handed down. The last time we tried to assign chores was three weeks earlier, when we concluded that the kids should take turns carrying out the garbage. Her 14-year-old immediately moved the bathroom scale into the kitchen so he could weigh the garbage every night and make sure his bag wasn't heavier than his brothers'.

That evening we assemble the kids in the kitchen.

"Your mother and I have decided it's time for you guys to start doing a little work around here," I tell them.

"I already do plenty of work," says the 13-year-old.

"Like what?"

"Almost every night I do the dishes after dinner."

"Putting your plate on the floor for the cat to lick is not doing the dishes," I rule. "Now, here's the way it's going to be and I'm not listening to any arguments. On Saturday mornings, you're all going to clean your rooms. The 13-year-old will vacuum the living room, the 14-year-old will dust the furniture and the 16-year-old will clean the upstairs bathroom."

The 16-year-old argues that he shouldn't have to clean the bathroom because he only goes at school. The 13-year-old argues that he'll get a hernia if he has to vacuum because the 14-year-old will push all the dust from the furniture onto the floor and he'll have to sweep it up. The 14-year-old races upstairs for the bathroom scale to see if his dust is going to weigh more than his brother's dust.

I adjourn the court and head for the bar.

But most of cases are not that complicated. Most of them are like the one that is presented to me when a 16-year-old defendant walks into the kitchen and offers, as his opening argument:

"He's lying."

"Who's lying?" I ask.

"The 13-year-old. He's lying through his teeth."

"How can he be lying? He's not even here."

"Yeah, I know. But he's gonna lie when he gets here."

A minute later the plaintiff appears in the kichen. He is holding his stomach and moaning. Either his brother has punched him or he is in the final stages of labor.

"What's the problem?" I inquire.

"He punched me," the 13-year-old moans.

I turn to the 16-year-old.

"Why did you punch him?"

"I didn't punch him. I barely touched him."

"What did you barely touch him with, an ax handle?"

"How come you always believe him and you never believe me?"

"Well, for one thing, I've known you three years longer. But I didn't say I don't believe you. So why don't you tell me exactly what happened?"

"OK," the 16-year-old says. "Here's what happened. I'm like, sitting at my desk, studying, when he comes into my room without knocking and starts dribbling his basketball right behind my chair for, like, about an hour. I ask him to please stop, but he won't stop. So I get up to go to the living room to study and I accidentally brush up against him."

I try to envision this sequence of events in my mind. I'm having trouble getting past the part where the 16-year-old is, like, studying.

"Your witness," I tell the 13-year-old.

"I go into his room to see if he wants to shoot some hoops," the 13-year-old testifies, "and the basketball slips out of my hands and lands on the floor. So he gets up and punches me in the stomach about a hundred times for no reason."

They look at me and wait for a decision. After hearing both sides, I have a pretty good idea of what really happened. The 13-year-old dribbled the ball once. The 16-year-old told him not to do it again or he'd punch his lights out. The 13-year-old called the 16-year-old a name. The 16-year-old punched him. And there wasn't an open school book in sight.

But in the absence of reliable eye witnesses, I am forced to render no verdict.

"Let's just forget about it," I say, turning back to the stove. "Dinner's almost ready. One of you set the table and the other one take out the garbage."

"I took the garbage out last time," a voice behind me shouts.

"No you didn't, jerk," a voice shouts back.

There is the sound of a scuffle. Followed by the sound of a punch. Followed by a moan.

Maybe it's not such a good idea to put parents on the Supreme Court, after all. Their first decision would be a unanimous vote for capital punishment.

## INGRATITUDE

There are many rewards in parenthood. Gratitude is not one of them.

You may, if you're lucky, get pride and joy from your children. But if it's appreciation you want, buy a cocker spaniel.

No sacrifice you make is too big for a kid to ignore. You can show him the stretch marks on your hips or the zeros in your bank account. He will not care. You can't shame a kid into appreciating what you do for him. If you mention your sacrifices, his answer will be, "I didn't ask you to have me."

I receive another generous dose of ingratitude one dark and stormy afternoon. The rain is pouring down outside my office. Lightning is ripping across the sky. But the 15-year-old has a basketball scrimmage in a gym two counties away and I have promised to be there.

(Being there is the cardinal rule of parenthood. If you miss even one of your child's activities, he or she automatically will become a mass murderer, a drug addict or a U.S. Senator. And it will be your fault.)

So I leave the office, pop my umbrella and head for the parking lot. The umbrella does a fair job of keeping the rain from falling on my head. Unfortunately, it's not real effective against the torrent of water flowing down the sidewalk and over my shoes.

I slosh my way to the parking lot, where I find that my car is up to its rocker panels in water on all sides. I have two choices. I can wade through the water to my car, or I can stand my ground and wait for my car to float to me.

The water is up to my shins as I splash to my car and get in. I gun the car through the puddle, spraying a rooster tail of water that scores a direct hit on a guy who is racing to his car. I feel bad about that. Then again, even *my* boss should be smart enough not to be outside on a day like this.

As I pull out of the lot, I turn the windshield wipers and the defroster on high. The wipers don't clear the water off the outside of the windshield, exactly. They just move it from one side to the other. Not that it matters. The defroster is doing absolutely nothing to keep the inside of the windshield clear. But it does direct a nice stream of cold air onto my wet feet.

With one hand on the wheel and the other smearing away the steam on the inside of the windshield, I make it to the highway. My car's headlights are feeble flickers in the storm's darkness. Fortunately, there is an enormous flash of lightning illuminating the road every few seconds.

As nearly as I can recall from my high school meteorology class, if lightning hits your car, all that will happen is that it will run across the top, down the sides and melt your tires. Which would be more comforting if I weren't driving a convertible. I don't think convertibles were covered in my high school meteorology class. My best guess is that, if lightning hits my convertible, it will set my top on fire and melt my head.

After a lifetime of driving, I reach the gym, hop out of the car and race into the building. Just inside the door I take off my shoes, remove my socks and roll my pants up to my knees. Barefoot, I hurry to the basketball court. I've made it in time. The 15-year-old's team still is warming up.

As I walk toward the bleachers, the 15-year-old spots me. Dropping his basketball, he runs to me. There is a look of distress on his face.

"Dad . . . " he begins.

"That's all right, son. It was a rough drive, but I made it."

" . . . you look like a dork," he continues. "Put your shoes and socks back on and roll your pants down. You're embarrassing me."

A cocker spaniel would have wagged its tail.

## MALINGERING

In 1989, the big news at the Academy Awards was Dustin Hoffman, who took a slender story about an autistic-savant and turned it into an Oscar-winning performance.

The acting was excellent, but no one at our house was all that impressed. That's because we know what *real* acting is. We have four kids who could take a sore throat and turn it into the deathbed scene from *La Boheme* . Without rehearsals, a script or an agent, they can take a 101-degree temperature and wring more pathos out of it than Meryl Streep on her best day.

One of the more memorable performances is turned in by the 14-year-old when he begins to complain about a sore throat. We take him to the doctor, who runs some tests and determines that he has strep throat.

We are concerned, but not worried. Among 14-year-olds, strep throats are about as common as dirty fingernails. A few days of rest, a pound of penicillin and he'll be back on his feet.

We take him home, give him a pill and prop him up on the living room couch with a blanket and enough videos to put Siskel and Ebert into a coma. Every 10 minutes his mother feels his forehead. Every 15 minutes she helps him sip a little orange juice.

For the next two days he remains on the couch, watching movies and sighing dramatically whenever either of us walks through the room. Just to sort of remind us he still is there, suffering bravely.

On the fourth day, when it is beginning to appear his greatest health risk is that he is going to become permanently grafted to the couch, I mention to his mother that he seems to be stretching this thing out a little bit.

"Strep throat can be serious," she replies. "I don't think we should rush him."

"Rush him? I've seen people who have recovered from open heart surgery faster than this."

"He still has a temperature."

"I know, I saw the thermometer. But in a recent survey of major Midwestern hospitals, nine out of 10 doctors agreed that a temperature of 98.7 is not life-threatening."

"He seems awfully listless."

"You'd be listeless, too, if you watched *Beetlejuice* 34 consecutive times in a four-day period."

"Well, maybe we could talk to him."

We go into the living room to talk to him. He sighs dramatically when he sees us coming. We see his lips move, but we cannot hear what he is saying. His mother puts her ear close to his mouth and listens.

"He wants you to rewind the tape," she tells me. As the videocassette is rewinding, his lips move again.

"He wants you to sit next to him on the couch and hold his eyelids open for him while he watches the movie," his mother says.

"That's it," I shout . "He's milking this thing too much. If we let him, he'll spend the rest of his life on that couch while we . . . "

My diagnosis is interrupted by the ringing of the phone. His mother answers it.

"No, John, I don't think he can come over today," she says into the phone. "He's very, very sick and . . . "

"Is that John?" the 14-year-old yells.

"He's getting up a soccer game, but I told him you were too . . . "

Before she can finish her sentence, the 14-year-old jumps off the couch, bounds upstairs in two leaps, grabs his cleats, shimmies down the drain pipe and disappears over the horizon.

In the living room, we settle back to watch Michael Keaton in *Beetlejuice.* He gives the second best performance we have seen all week.

## PROCRASTINATION

It took the ancient Egyptians 20 years to build the Great Pyramid of

Khufu. I think I know why it too so long. Khufu spent the first 19 years trying to get his kids to help him.

The surest way to turn a chore into a career is to let a kid get involved. As I prove once again on the spring morning I decide it is time to plant a few tomatoes. It should be, I estimate, a two-hour job. All we have to do is rake a handful of dead leaves, turn the soil and put the seedlings into the ground.

"If we all pitch in and do this together," I tell my kids, "we'll be done by noon and have the rest of the weekend free to enjoy. So let's get going."

"OK," agrees the 16-year-old, "I'll help you as soon as I eat some breakfast."

"And I have to get dressed," says the 14-year-old.

"Can I finish playing this video game?" asks the 13-year-old. "I just have one man left."

"Fine," I agree. "I'll go outside and get started. You guys come out as soon as you're ready."

While they are inside dressing, eating and gaming, I rake the dead leaves out of the tomato bed, turn the soil, plant the seedlings, fertilize them, water them and build cages around them. The first kid has yet to make an appearance on the patio. By the time they get out here, I am beginning to suspect, little yellow flowers will be appearing on those plants. I go inside to investigate.

The 16-year-old is standing at the stove, stirring something in a pan.

"Hey, I thought you were going to come out and help me when you got done with breakfast," I say.

"I am," he says. "The hollandaise sauce is almost ready."

"Why are you making hollandaise sauce?"

"You don't expect me to make eggs Benedict without hollandaise sauce, do you?"

"I didn't expect you to make eggs Benedict at all. When you said you were going to make breakfast, I thought you were going to have a vat of Wheaties or a couple dozen packages of Pop Tarts like you usually do."

"Breakfast is the most important meal of the day," he says.

"Thank you very much, Betty Crocker. Where's your stepbrother?"

"He's upstairs, getting dressed. " I head upstairs. The 14-year-old is in the bathroom. Blow-drying his hair.

"What are you doing?" I demand.

"If I don't blow-dry my hair right after I get out of the shower, I can't do a thing with it."

"Let me see if I have this straight. You had to take a shower and wash your hair before you could come outside and dig rocks out of the garden?"

"Cleanliness is next to godliness," he says. "Would you hand me that can of mousse?"

I head back downstairs. The 13-year-old is on the floor in front of the television, zapping dragons with his joystick.

"I thought you only had one man left," I say.

"I did," he says. "But just before he died he discovered the passage to the secret kingdom of Xernon and I got 43 free men and 100 million bonus points. This is the best game I've ever had."

I give up and head back outside. By the time one of these kids actually shows up on the patio, there will be large, red tomatoes on my plants . And if he had waited for his kids to help build his pyramid, I'm pretty sure, Khufu would have wound up being buried in a Hefty bag.

As good as they are at stalling, I'll have to admit, my teen-agers are amateurs compared with the 11-year-old. The next time you find yourself on death row and your lawyer has run out of appeals, call on him. The kid will come up with enough excuses to keep you healthy until the 22nd Century. Not only will he keep you out of the chair, he'll find loopholes to guarantee that never again will you have to clean your room, do the dishes or eat asparagus.

He does his best work at bedtime, which is supposed to be 9 p.m. on weeknights, but always turns out to be more like the following itinerary:

**9 p.m.** — The 11-year-old is sitting in front of the television.

"It's 9 o'clock," I announce. "Do you know where your bedroom is?"

"Can I just watch the end of this?" he asks, his eyes never leaving the screen. "I've been waiting all week to see it."

"It's a dog food commercial."

"Yeah. But I want to see how it turns out."

"The dog eats his food and lives to be 48 years old. Now go to bed."

**9:01** — The 11-year-old walks upstairs. It takes him two minutes per step.

**9:25** — A voice calls down from upstairs.

"Does anybody know where the dictionary is?"

"Why?"

"I hafta write a book report. It's due tomorrow morning."

"Why didn't you do it earlier?"

"I forgot."

It is not a very satisfactory answer. But then, it was a silly question.

**9:26** — The 11-year-old is in the dining room, starting his book report.

**9:27** — The 11-year-old is in the kitchen, drinking a Coke.

"I thought you had a book report to do," I say.

"All that writing made me thirsty."

**9:34** — The 11-year-old has finished with his book report. He heads back upstairs. It takes him three minutes per step.

**10:10** — A voice calls from upstairs.

"Was I supposed to take a shower tonight?"

"I don't know," I admit. "Did you take one last night?"

"I forget."

"How about the night before?"
"I can't remember."
"When's the last time you *do* remember taking a shower?"
"Christmas Eve."
"Take a shower."
**10:12** — The shower begins to run.
**10:21** — The shower continues to run.
**10:35** — The shower still is running. Water tables as far away as British Columbia are approaching drought level.
**10:38** — The 11-year-old is standing in the living room. Dripping.
"Why aren't you in bed?" I ask.
"I forgot to kiss everybody goodnight."
He kisses every lip in the room and heads back upstairs.
**10:39** — The 11-year-old is back in the living room.
"I forgot to kiss the cat."
**10:40** — A voice calls from upstairs.
"I can't get to sleep. What should I do?"
"Try counting something."
"Like what?'
"How about the number of times you've been up and down the stairs tonight?"
**11:30** — I turn off the television and head upstairs to bed. In the hallway, I encounter the 11-year-old.
"Now what?"
"Bathroom," he says.
I shrug and head for the bedroom. I'd like to make sure the kid gets to bed at a decent hour. But who can stay up that late?

## SCHIZOPHRENIA

In spite of what most people believe, *Dr. Jekyll and Mr. Hyde* is not a work of fiction that sprang from the imagination of Robert Louis Stevenson. It is a true story, based on his 13-year-old.

Every 13-year-old is schizophrenic. The world may see a Dr. Jekyll. But his parents live with a creature who has fangs, long black fingernails and hair sprouting out of his forehead. If you don't believe that, it's only because it's been too long since the last time you went to a school open house.

The last time I went to my 13-year-old's open house, I stood in the doorway of his classroom and carefully checked out his teacher from a distance. When I was sure that he was not armed, I figured it was safe to approach him and tell him which 13-year-old I belong to.

"Oh, yes," his teacher says, "he's a delightful child."

"You must have misunderstood," I say, repeating the 13-year-old's name and being careful to stay out of arm's reach.

"Sure, sure, I know who he is," the teacher smiles. "He's a pleasure to have in my class."

Suddenly I realize what is happening here. This is an open house. On open house days, teachers start their mornings with a hearty bowl of Quaaludes so they can say nice things to parents about their children. At a junior high open house in the 4th Century, I'm willing to bet there was a teacher who said, "It's very nice to meet you, Mr. Hun. Attila is such a pleasure to have in class. He shows definite leadership qualities."

"Look," I say, pulling the teacher aside, "you don't have to play this game with me. I know this kid and there are prison guards in Attica who would be afraid to turn their backs on him."

"I wouldn't know about that," his teacher says. "But here at school he doesn't give me a moment's trouble."

"Think carefully," I urge him. "The kid we're talking about is 5-foot-3, has enough nervous energy to light up Manhattan, talks loud enough to jam radar and could take on Melvin Belli and F. Lee Bailey in a tag-team debate."

"He *is* very lively," the teacher acknowledges. "He's all boy."

"Jesse James was all boy. This kid could wear out the Washington Redskins. Tell the truth, what do you use to get him to sit still for more than five minutes? A whip and a chair?"

"He always sits at his desk very quietly."

"Don't give me that. Nikon doesn't make a camera with a shutter speed fast enough to get a picture of that kid sitting still. If he's not jumping out of his seat every 30 seconds it means either you've got him strapped to his desk or he's in a coma."

"Well, you can check for yourself," his teacher says. "His desk is right over there and you can see there are no straps attached to it."

He points to a desk on the other side of the room. On top of the desk, three books are stacked in alphabetical order. Next to the books are half a dozen sharpened pencils in a precise row.

"Hold it," I say. "That's not his desk. Nothing he ever occupied for more than five minutes looked that neat. In fact, the reason his mother isn't here tonight is because she went into his bedroom three days ago to change his sheets and she hasn't been heard from since. At this very moment there's a rescue crew at our house trying to dig a tunnel through the dirty underwear to reach her."

"His desk isn't always that tidy," the teacher admits. "Sometimes, after he gets done erasing blackboards, emptying wastebaskets and picking up after his classmates, he doesn't have time to clean his desk before the bell rings."

"You've found some way to force him to work?"

"He volunteers."

I can't take any more. I thank the teacher, walk to the cafeteria, find the 13-year-old who is quiet, polite and hard-working and we leave the school building. As we are walking through the parking lot, hairs start sprouting from the kid's forehead.

**SLOTH**

When I was a kid, summer vacation was too valuable to waste on anything as useless as sleeping.

Every morning from June to September I would leap out of bed, wake up the roosters, hop on my bike and pedal off to find the nearest vacant lot, where I would spend all morning playing baseball. I had more strike-outs by 9 a.m. than most people had all day.

Kids in the digital generation apparently are operating with an entirely different biological clock.

On a warm summer day, for example, I stop home for lunch at 12:30 in the afternoon. The television screen is blank, all six CD players are silent and every light in the house is off. There can be only one explanation: Power outage.

I locate my wife in the backyard.

"I thought I'd come home and have lunch with my little family," I tell her. "Where are the kids?"

"If you're referring to the Van Winkle stepbrothers," she says, "they're sleeping."

"Aren't they a little old for naps?"

"What naps? They haven't gotten up yet."

"You mean they've been sleeping all day?"

"Not necessarily," she says. "One of them must have gotten out of bed sometime this morning. The toilet seat is up."

"Don't you think you should do something about it?"

"I *am* doing something about it. Every two hours I go up to their rooms and hold a mirror under their noses."

"I was thinking more along the lines of making them get up," I suggest.

"This job doesn't pay enough to make me go back up and try to get them out of bed while the sun's still shining," she says. "The only way you're going to get those kids out of bed is to set fire to their pillows."

"Getting them up doesn't have to be a battle," I point out. "You just have to be firm about it."

"Fine. *You* go in and get them up."

I march upstairs to the 16-year-old's room and rap on the door.

"Hey, Rip Van Teen-ager, it's time to get up," I announce, firmly.

"What time is it?"

"July."

"How long have I been sleeping?"

"Let me put it this way. Since the last time you were in a vertical position, Bart Simpson has been elected president, Michael Jackson has grown a beard and every rap group in America has gone to jail."

"You're putting me on about Bart Simpson, right?"

"Why don't you get up and see for yourself, dude?"

"This is my vacation. I'm supposed to relax."

"Have it your way," I tell him. "But if you don't get up right away you're going to suffer irreversible bed hair and you'll never be able to comb it again."

The next blur I see is the 16-year-old heading for his mousse.

I head for the 14-year-old's room.

"Get up," I yell, "you're missing puberty."

"I don't hafta get up," a voice mumbles from underneath a mound of blankets. "It's summer vacation."

"This isn't a vacation, it's a hibernation. At this very moment your mother is at the grocery store buying roots and grubs in preparation for the day you come out of your cave."

"Why should I get up?" the voice argues. "There's no school, I'm too young to get a job and there's nothing good on television until tonight." The fact that the voice is arguing with me does not necessarily mean that the 14-year-old is awake. We're talking about a kid who argued with a nurse during his tonsillectomy.

He burrows deeper under his covers like a teen-age mutant ninja mole.

"Well, it's up to you, I suppose," I tell him. "But I think it's only fair to let you know that your stepbrother is up already and he's headed for the last package of Pop Tarts in the kitchen." Quick reflexes keep me from being trampled by 14-year-old bare feet.

There's a time to be firm and there's a time to be devious. Parenthood is the perfect time to be devious.

## UNCONSCIOUSNESS

When we took delivery of them, all our kids appeared to be factory-equipped with the standard features: Ten tiny little fingers, 10 precious little toes and all five senses.

Now they have a few miles on them. Their tiny little fingers have left smudges on every mirror, window and ceiling in the house. The tiny little toes poke through the end of a new pair of Nikes approximately every two weeks. And most of their senses haven't worked in years.

The 16-year-old, for instance, no longer can see.

I become aware of his failing eyesight when I notice that the trash can in the kitchen overfloweth. I stuff the trash into a plastic bag and set it squarely in front of the kitchen door to be taken out by the next kid who goes to the backyard.

Two hours later, the 16-year-old has gone in and out of the kitchen seven times and the trash bag still is in front of the door.

"When are you going to take out the trash?" I ask him, finally.

"What trash?"

"The trash sitting in the plastic bag in the kitchen."

"I didn't see it."

"How could you not see it? You've gone to the backyard seven times since I put it there. To get to the backyard, you either had to move the trash out of the way or you climbed out your bedroom window, walked across the roof, slid down the drain . . . "

While we are discussing the possibilities, the phone begins to ring in the living room. I leave the kitchen and walk to the living room. The phone is on the end table. Which is next to the couch. Which is occupied by the 14-year-old.

"Why don't you answer the phone?" I ask him.

"What phone?"

"The phone that's ringing six inches from your head."

I grab the phone on its 17th ring, say hello, listen for a minute, then hang up.

"Who was it?" the 14-year-old asks.

"It was John calling for you."

"Why didn't you hand me the phone?"

"What for? You wouldn't have been able to hear him anyway."

This conversation is interrupted by the entrance of the 13-year-old, waving a sandwich.

"What's wrong with this bologna?" he demands. "It tastes funny."

"That's because it's corned beef," I reply.

"Are you sure?"

"Positive. Bologna doesn't have fat around the edges."

"Maybe it'll taste better with more catsup on it."

He heads back to the kitchen. I head upstairs. At the top of the stairs I notice an unpleasant aroma coming from beneath the 11-year-old's bedroom door. I take a deep breath and open it. The odor is coming from the cat's litter box.

"When are you going to clean that litter box?" I ask the 11-year-old.

"Why, what's wrong with it?" he asks.

"It's giving off fumes. Don't tell me you can't smell them."

"I smelled something," he admits, "but I thought it was coming from the 14-year-old's clothes hamper. Anyway, it's not that bad."

"Then why is the cat wearing a gas mask?"

"I wondered about that," he admits.

I close his door, head for my room and lock myself inside. My kids are losing their senses, one by one. I, on the other hand, am in danger of taking leave of all mine at the same time.

# The Last Word On Stepfatherhood

A friend of mine is getting married soon. It is his first trip down the aisle, but the bride has been there before and she has two teen-age children to prove it.

I'm happy for all of them. But I don't envy the man.

I had 13 years to prepare myself for my first teen-ager and longer than that to prepare me for stepchildren. It still wasn't enough. This guy is going into the job with a blank resume and an empty portfolio. There's really nothing I can say to make it easier for him. Parenthood is the ultimate in on-the-job training.

But at least I can pass along a few tips:

• Kiss your clothes goodbye. Sweaters will disappear. Shirts will vanish. Tennis shoes will go AWOL and not return to active duty until the tread is gone and there are holes in the toes. But if it's really important to you to find out what happened to your last pair of clean socks, go into your stepson's room and look under his bed. Hold your breath first.

• Kiss your favorite radio stations goodbye. It's like the old *Outer Limits* television show. No one ever sees it happen, but somehow an unseen force takes control of your car radio dial when you have teen-agers. After that, the only stations you will be able to receive will be named Z-something and will be operated by disc jockeys who think Mozart, Frank Sinatra and the Beatles all were contemporaries.

• For the rest of your life do not expect to receive any telephone messages. No matter how important you think your phone calls are, to your stepchildren they merely will be annoying interruptions between *their* phone calls. On a good day, they may remember to tell you that there was a call for you. But don't expect them to remember such minor details as who it was, when they called, why they called or whether they were a man or a woman. In the ears of a teen-ager, a phone call from George Bush is nothing more than "some guy who sounds like Dana Carvey called."

• Be aware that, for a man with a family, there is no such thing as "an inexpensive restaurant." Donald Trump may once have been able to pay cash for a 75-foot yacht, but he never had enough money in his wallet to cover the cost of buying soft drinks for a tableful of teen-agers.

• Check out the location of your nearest video rental store. It is less expensive to *make* a movie than it is to take them to one.

• When your wife brings home the groceries, do not look at the bottom line of the cash register receipt unless you have written permission from your cardiologist.

• If you find something you like in the refrigerator, eat it now. The leftover pizza you were planning to warm up for a midnight snack will never make it past 8 p.m. if a kid spots it.

• Just say no. It doesn't matter how innocuous a kid's request might seem on the surface. In the long run, it's going to cost you money.

• Invest heavily in power company stock. That will ease the pain when you come home and find that the television, the air conditioner, three stereos and every light in the place have been turned on. By kids who left the house three hours ago.

And try to remember that:

• Just because your stepchildren do not hear you when you ask them to take out the garbage does not mean that they are deaf.

• Just because your stepchildren cannot see two bath towels, four empty soft drink cans and six weeks' worth of dirty underwear lying on the floor when you ask them to clean their rooms does not mean that they are blind.

• Just because your stepchildren cannot remember a homework assignment until the night before it is due, a soccer practice until 10 minutes before it is scheduled to start or a dentist's appointment until three days after it was scheduled does not mean that they have Adolescent Alzheimer's Disease.

It just means that they are normal.

Well, typical, anyway.